# Buildings

# That Breathe

GREENING

THE

WORLD'S

CITIES

NANCY F. CASTALDO

TWENTY-FIRST CENTURY BOOKS / MINNEAPOLIS

*For Dean, "E quindi uscimmo a riveder le stelle"*

Twenty-First Century Books™
An imprint of Lerner Publishing Group, Inc.
241 First Avenue North
Minneapolis, MN 55401 USA

For reading levels and more information, look up this title at www.lernerbooks.com.

Diagrams on pages 11 and 50 by Laura K. Westlund.
Main body text set in Adobe Garamond Pro.
Typeface provided by Adobe Systems.

**Library of Congress Cataloging-in-Publication Data**

Names: Castaldo, Nancy F. (Nancy Fusco), 1962– author.
Title: Buildings that breathe : greening the world's cities / Nancy F. Castaldo.
Description: Minneapolis : Twenty-First Century Books, [2023] | Includes bibliographical references and index. | Audience: Ages 13–18 | Audience: Grades 10–12 | Summary: "Urban planners, architects, and scientists are developing high-rise forests that seek to balance human activity and natural regeneration. Discover how green infrastructure will transform the urban landscape and how we think about our future"— Provided by publisher.
Identifiers: LCCN 2022004028 (print) | LCCN 2022004029 (ebook) | ISBN 9781728419466 (lib. bdg.) | ISBN 9781728462691 (eb pdf)
Subjects: LCSH: Municipal engineering. | Sustainable urban development. | Sustainable architecture. | Environmental protection.
Classification: LCC TD159 .C37 2023  (print) | LCC TD159  (ebook) | DDC 628—dc23/eng/20220414

LC record available at https://lccn.loc.gov/2022004028
LC ebook record available at https://lccn.loc.gov/2022004029

Manufactured in the United States of America
1-49069-49267-5/16/2022

# Contents

At Bosco Verticale in Milan, Italy, more than sixteen thousand plants and trees grow on balconies and other areas of two residential towers.

The goal of life is living in agreement with nature.

—Zeno, Greek philosopher, circa 450 BCE

# CHAPTER 1

# Greening Our Cities

Do you live or go to school in a city full of tall buildings and paved sidewalks? If so, look outside your window. What do you see? You might see the concrete wall of a skyscraper, a fire escape, or rooftops. No matter where you live, imagine instead looking out upon branches full of leaves, as if you were standing in a forest. Imagine looking out from a treescraper.

Pretend you're taking an elevator inside this treescraper. The door opens to a floor of apartments. Each of them has a terrace with views unlike those of other apartment buildings. The terraces are alive. They are shaded by branches filled with green leaves and nesting birds. Blooms fill the air with sweetness. For residents, it's almost like living in a treehouse. The place invites visitors and residents to take a deep breath, sit down, and relax. Could this treescraper exist in a congested city? Yes, it can—and it does.

Milan, a city in northern Italy, is home to two innovative green towers called Bosco Verticale. That's Italian for "vertical forest." The complex, in the heart of a bustling European city with a train station just steps away, was designed by Italian architect Stefano Boeri. The two treescrapers not only please residents but also help the entire city. These are buildings filled with trees and plants, which release the life-giving gas oxygen and absorb the gas carbon dioxide. They are buildings that breathe.

## CITY LIFE

Cities are one of the most complex inventions of civilization. They are filled with libraries, schools, museums, factories, and restaurants. They bring people together to socialize and do business. In cities, people collaborate and share ideas. Ed Glaeser, an economist at Harvard University, describes cities as "places of competition . . . places of innovation."

But these population centers have many downsides. For instance, they produce three-quarters of the world's carbon dioxide. This gas traps heat from the sun, much like the glass roof and walls of a greenhouse trap the sun's heat. Carbon dioxide occurs naturally on Earth, but humans add extra carbon dioxide to the air when they burn fossil fuels (coal, oil, and natural gas). By driving gasoline-powered vehicles, heating homes and businesses with oil and gas, and powering factories and machines with fossil fuels, humans add more than 44 billion tons (40 billion t) of carbon dioxide to the air each year. All this heat-trapping gas has raised temperatures on Earth and changed Earth's climate. The excess heat is causing powerful storms and weather disasters such as droughts (periods with little or no rainfall), floods, and wildfires. The heat is also melting ice at the North and South Poles. As the ice melts, sea levels rise, threatening to flood coastal cities and engulf low-lying islands.

Many big cities are crowded and polluted. Green buildings and other green spaces can improve life for city residents.

Besides releasing carbon dioxide, the cars, factories, homes, and businesses in big cities do additional damage. They create other types of pollution, such as nitrogen dioxide, sulfur dioxides, and particulate matter, or small airborne particles, such as soot from smokestacks. According to the World Health Organization (WHO), an international agency devoted to improving human health, 91 percent of the world's population breathes unhealthy air. About nine million people die every year from air-pollution–related illnesses, such as strokes, heart disease, and lung disease.

The entire Earth is warming, but even without climate change, cities are warmer than nonurban areas, such as farms and forests. Rural areas have an abundance of natural features that cool the air, including green plants, shade-giving trees, and wetlands. With their paved roads and big buildings, cities have far fewer green spaces and natural bodies of water. Pavement and roofing materials absorb and emit the sun's heat, making cities even hotter. Cars, air-conditioning units, and other machines also generate heat. In a big metropolis, such as New York City, temperatures in summer can be about 7°F (4°C) higher than in areas outside the city. Because cities are so much hotter than the surrounding countryside, they are called heat islands.

The pollution and temperature of cities impact everyone, not just the millions of people who live and work within them. Air pollution doesn't just stay within city limits. It travels with the wind to all parts of Earth. And climate change affects every living thing on Earth. In many places, the air and ocean have become too warm for some plants and animals. Floods, droughts, and other weather disasters hurt wildlife too. Pollution of both air and water also harms and kills many plants and animals.

In 2018 about 55 percent of Earth's people lived in cities. The United Nations, an international humanitarian and peacekeeping organization, predicted that by 2050 that number would grow to about 68 percent. With the world's population increasing, cities will only get bigger, hotter, and more polluted. What is the solution? There is no one easy answer. But green buildings such as Bosco Verticale could play an important role.

## PLANNING FOR CHANGE

In 2018 scientists, urban planners, architects, and foresters from ninety-three countries, including Bosco Verticale designer Stefano Boeri, gathered in the small city of Mantua, Italy, to discuss how they could contribute to creating greener cities. At the conference, called the World Forum on Urban Forests, these experts discussed projects in place and future projects that could help stem climate change, reduce pollution, combat increased temperatures, and protect wildlife.

Together such experts are working toward a new era of urban greening. This work involves planting more trees, creating more urban green spaces, and integrating more plants into architectural designs. Greening cities benefits residents in many ways. In a 2016 study on urban green spaces and health, researchers at WHO found evidence that urban green spaces help residents sleep better and stay healthier. That's because trees and plants help us relax. Parks and other green spaces give people places to walk, play, and exercise. They provide homes for birds and other animals. In cities with a lot of greenery, the sounds of birds, wind, water, and wildlife can help drown out the aggravating noise of cars and industry. Green spaces also provide us with inspiration and a sense of well-being.

Architect Stefano Boeri stands on a balcony at Bosco Verticale.

Following the World Forum on Urban Forests, Boeri gave a presentation called "City Vision: Vertical Forests" at the 2018 *New York Times* Cities for Tomorrow conference. In his talk, he called climate change and pollution an enemy and said that moving "the forests inside the city is an attempt to fight the enemy in its battlefield." He hopes that trees and forests "will become an integral part of the life sphere of millions of citizens in the world."

Urban trees provide shade and can also capture air and water pollution.

## WHY TREES?

Trees provide our world with countless benefits. They provide habitats, or homes, for many organisms, from the tiniest ant to frogs, birds, and mammals. They provide fruits, syrup, nuts, medicines, and much more for wildlife and humans. They also provide humans with wood, rubber, paper, and other substances used to make buildings and household products. Tree roots anchor the soil from erosion, keeping it from washing away in floods or blowing away in the wind. Trees also release oxygen, a gas that animals need to survive. Their canopies (spreading branches) lower temperatures and supply shade, reducing the temperature of urban heat islands. The Food and Agriculture Organization of the United Nations says that trees in urban areas can cool the air by between 3.6°F and 14.4°F (2°C and 8°C).

Because trees absorb carbon dioxide and emit oxygen, people compare them to human lungs (which take in oxygen and release carbon dioxide).

## Carbon In, Oxygen Out

Trees and other green plants absorb carbon dioxide and make their food during a process called photosynthesis. Their leaves absorb light from the sun and carbon dioxide from the air. Plant roots take in water, which travels through the plant to the leaves. Inside the leaves, raw materials break down and combine to make glucose, which plants use as food. Photosynthesis also releases oxygen from the water. Plants expel the oxygen through tiny holes in their leaves, providing the essential gas that humans and almost all other animals need to live.

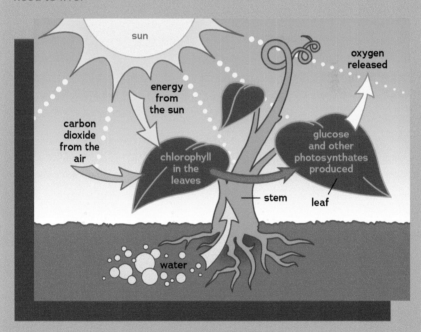

But trees can also be compared to human livers. The liver traps poisons, chemicals, and other harmful substances that enter the human body. It processes these substances, allowing them to exit the body through urine and feces. Similarly, trees trap pollution from the air. Leaves absorb gaseous pollutants like sulfur dioxide and nitrogen dioxide. These substances often don't harm trees, but they can harm humans. Leaves also trap dust, ash, and smoke, substances that aren't good for trees, humans, or any living things. Tree roots, in addition to anchoring the soil, can trap polluted water from farms and cities, keeping it from running off into lakes and rivers.

One of the most important ways that trees fight climate change is by absorbing carbon dioxide. Trees need carbon dioxide to make food. They store it in their stems and leaves as they grow. According to the United States Department of Agriculture (USDA), a mature tree absorbs more than 48 pounds (22 kg) of carbon dioxide each year. When people cut down trees to build houses, farms, roads, and other structures, they eliminate these vital climate change fighters. When people cut down large tracts of forest—called deforestation—they contribute to climate change on an even bigger scale. But when people plant trees—whether on a small scale or a large scale—they help fight climate change.

Planting trees anywhere—but especially in cities—is a simple yet powerful action to help protect Earth and its living things. While trees might not stop climate change altogether, they might slow it down. They can also help protect the water we drink and the air we breathe.

## IS THERE A DOWNSIDE?

Nothing is perfect, and that applies to planting trees too. While trees are great at sucking up pollution, this isn't a good thing for some tree species. Some pollutants can damage or kill the trees themselves. Trees can also trap pollution near the ground, where it can harm human health.

## Cut Down Usage or Cut Down Trees

While greening our cities is a great way to return trees to our planet, make our cities healthier, and slow climate change, it doesn't replace the need for forest preservation. Natural forests are home to many old and ancient trees. Saving these forests not only combats climate change and provides us with life-sustaining oxygen, but it also preserves the habitats of the plants and animals that live there. In 2012 the United Nations declared March 21 as the International Day of Forests to raise awareness about the importance of all kinds of forests.

One way to protect natural forests is to reduce usage of tree-based products. Humans use trees to make everything from furniture to toilet paper. Even the paper in this book comes from trees. Countless trees are cut down to meet the demand for paper and wood products. Using fewer of these products lowers that demand and can save trees from clear-cutting.

Young people around the world have stepped up to protect forests and plant new trees. Inspired by Kenyan environmental activist and tree planter Wangari Maathai, Felix Finkbeiner of Germany began his tree-planting mission at nine years old. He developed Plant-for-the-Planet, an initiative to encourage kids to restore forests by planting trees. More than ninety thousand youths in seventy-five countries are involved with his organization. Their goal is to plant one trillion trees. You can join the effort by planting trees or protecting a local forest.

Here are more simple steps that help to preserve natural forests:

- Use less paper.
- Choose recycled paper.
- Use tree-free products.
- Explore the origin of the wood you buy to make sure it is sustainably harvested.
- Support forest conservation organizations.
- Become an activist and communicate with elected officials about the need to save our forests.

Some people are allergic to certain trees, and falling tree branches can also endanger people and property. But scientists say that overall, trees are good for human health. For instance, a 2008 WHO report found that children living in an area of New York City with a lot of trees had fewer cases of asthma than those living in parts of the city without trees. One of the biggest takeaways from WHO's 2016 urban study was that the benefits of green spaces far outweigh the problems.

## Super City Tree

Polluted air and water can be toxic to trees as well as people, so not all trees can thrive in a crowded, dirty city. High amounts of pollution from buildings and cars can stress trees and even kill them. When they plant trees in urban areas, arborists, or tree doctors, and botanists choose tree species that are pollution-resistant—or able to absorb large amounts of pollution without getting sick themselves. The London plane tree (*Platanus acerifolia*) has a strong resistance to pollution. During the Industrial Revolution (late 1700s–early 1800s), when factories were first built in the cities of Europe and North America, Londoners realized that this tree could thrive even amid the smoke and grime of their city. So they planted the trees in large numbers. Now, more than half of the city's trees are London plane trees. People also planted London plane trees in other big cities, including Paris and New York City. You might be surprised to learn that this species, isn't actually native to London or even Europe. This famous smog-sucking tree is actually a hybrid of two trees from separate continents—the Oriental plane (*Platanus orientalis*) from Asia and the American sycamore (*Platanus occidentalis*) from North America.

## THE GREEN BUILDERS

The greening of cities doesn't involve only treescrapers like Bosco Verticale, where trees grow on big terraces built into each floor of the structure. Architects, botanists, and others are also planting trees and plants on rooftops and on building walls—both inside and outside. Some farmers are even creating vertical farms, where crops are grown on columns or shelves inside tall buildings. Green office buildings are becoming more common. For instance, in Seattle, Washington, the Spheres, a complex of large domes, provides a green workspace for eight hundred employees of the e-retailer Amazon. The Spheres includes forty thousand plants from about four hundred different species.

At the Spheres in Seattle, Amazon staffers work among thousands of green plants and trees.

Urban greening projects are even popping up in the movies. If you look carefully, you might spot images of Bosco Verticale and other green buildings in Wakanda, the fictional country in the film *Black Panther*. Environmentalist and urban ecologist C.N.E. Corbin, PhD, as a graduate student at the University of California–Berkeley, believed that this vision of the future can "both steer and stir us into thinking differently about cities, urban green spaces, neighborhoods, and our future."

## MILAN LEADING THE WAY

Milan is leading the world in urban greening. Like most cities, Milan faces many challenges. Its growing population and substantial industry have led to an unhealthy rise in air pollution and heat. Milan is one of the most polluted cities in Europe.

For a time, Milan was home to the famous artist and inventor Leonardo da Vinci (1452–1519). He lived during the Renaissance, a period of great cultural growth in Europe. Milan is entering a new era of innovation. According to Boeri, "The future of cities is an opportunity for a new Renaissance." He has taken the lead with Bosco Verticale. Completed in 2014, it contains 750 trees and more than five thousand other plants in its two apartment towers. The buildings—one with nineteen stories and the other with twenty-seven—provide an urban habitat for humans as well as plants, birds, and insects. The plants produce oxygen and provide shade for apartment dwellers.

When it comes to fighting climate change, deforestation, and other human-made problems, Boeri believes that vertical forests are part of the solution. "We have entered a new phase of human history, in which we will finally see a new alliance between forests and cities, two environments that our species has always kept separate," he says. "Trees and woods will no longer be just a decorative presence or a natural environment to be [limited to] protected areas, they will become an integral part of the life sphere of millions of citizens in the world. Protecting forests, reforesting cities and growing newly founded Forest-Cities: these are the great challenges to be faced immediately, all together."

# CHAPTER 2

# Green Cities Then and Now

**Urban greening is not new.** The city of Lucca, Italy, about three hours from Milan, is more than two thousand years old. To protect it from enemy armies, its early leaders surrounded it with thick earthen walls. In the 1500s, city leaders made the walls much thicker and stronger to protect the city from powerful enemy cannonballs. But the big walls—about 98 feet (30 m) wide and 39 feet (12 m) tall—served another purpose too. They were as wide as roads, so city leaders built tree-lined walkways on the top, planted with London plane, lime, holm oak, chestnut, and other tree species. At first, only nobles were allowed on this green path. But in 1815, Duchess María Luisa of Bourbon became the leader of Lucca. She made the path into a public walkway, accessible to all of Lucca's residents. In the twenty-first century, people living in Lucca still use and enjoy this pleasant green space.

In earlier centuries, city walls protected Lucca, Italy, from enemy attackers. In modern times, the walls serve as a park for city residents.

## TREES FOR HEALTH

In the nineteenth century, many American cities planted trees to improve life and health for residents. New York City is an example. The city's population exploded in the nineteenth century. By 1850 New York was home to nearly six hundred thousand people. Many neighborhoods were dirty and crowded, with few trees lining the streets. During this period, the city built its famous Central Park, in an area of the city called Seneca Village. The residents of this predominately Black community were forced to leave to make room for the park. The park's architect, Frederick Law Olmsted, said the space would "provide a natural verdant [green] and sylvan [wooded] scenery for the refreshment of town-strained men, women, and children." Central Park was completed in 1858.

## Remembering a Community: Seneca Village

About 225 Black, Irish, and German New Yorkers lived in Seneca Village between 1825 and 1857. For many, the community was a refuge from the racism and unhealthy living conditions that existed in other parts of New York. In addition to houses, Seneca Village had a school, three churches, and five cemeteries.

Using the law of eminent domain, which allows government to take private property for public use, the city acquired Seneca Village to build Central Park. Property owners were compensated for their losses, though many claimed their land was undervalued, resulting in the city paying them less than their property was worth. The homes were then knocked down to prepare for the construction of Central Park. After 140 years, city officials finally erected a marker in the park to commemorate Seneca Village. Since then, three archaeological excavations have recovered artifacts such as buttons, dishes, a toothbrush, and part of a child's shoe. These common items remind us of the families that thrived there before Central Park.

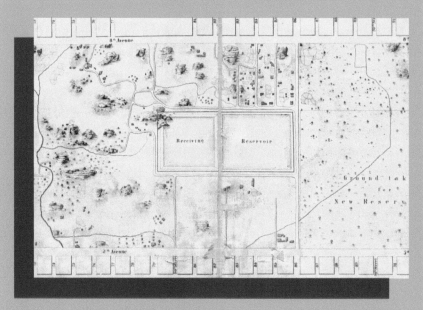

In the 1870s, Stephen Smith, a New York City doctor and founder of the city's Metropolitan Board of Health, led a push to plant more trees in the city. He argued that the trees would reduce New York's oppressive summer heat, release large amounts of oxygen, and improve the health of residents. To convince other city leaders of the wisdom of his idea, Smith pointed to a study conducted by Harvard University mathematician Benjamin Peirce.

Peirce's study focused on a famous elm tree in Boston, Massachusetts. Called the Washington Elm, it had an estimated seven million leaves. Peirce said that if all the leaves were laid out below the tree, they would cover 5 acres (2 ha) of ground. A tree with so many leaves had great potential for releasing life-giving oxygen. The leaves and branches also provided shade that offset the city's heat. The benefits of a single tree were enormous.

In 1873 Smith asked the New York State Legislature to establish a state bureau of forestry, but that didn't happen until 1902. Meanwhile, Smith and others joined together and formed the Tree Planting Association. They raised funds for tree planting and encouraged city residents to plant trees in front of their homes, apartments, and schools.

English urban planner Sir Ebenezer Howard also promoted tree planting. In 1898 he published *To-Morrow: A Peaceful Path to Real Reform* (republished in 1902 as *Garden Cities of To-Morrow*). The book described a new relationship between urban centers and nature. As a resident of the very dirty and crowded city of London, Howard imagined something better, greener, and healthier. His pie-shaped city plan was a perfect mix of urban and country living. It contained a center garden surrounded by houses, buildings, and parks arranged in concentric circles. His garden city would be populated by around thirty-two thousand people, with most traveling on foot and with very few cars. Howard made his plan come to life in east-central England. He and some business partners bought land around the village of

Large-scale tree farming is destructive to forest ecosystems.

Letchworth and in 1903 created Letchworth Garden City, with many of the features Howard described in his book.

## TEN TREES FOR EVERY CAR

Over the coming decades, cities grew, industry expanded, and more and more people traveled by car. In 1958 the president of the American Association for the Advancement of Science, medical doctor Chauncey D. Leake, first warned about global warming, which leads to climate change. He presented a paper detailing Earth's warming climate at the National Conference on Air Pollution. Leake recommended planting trees to offset the large amounts of carbon dioxide that humans were releasing into the air from cars, factories, and homes. Trees, he wrote, would store the extra carbon and absorb harmful air pollution. His plans were specific. He said that people should plant ten trees for every car on Earth and one hundred trees for every truck. Leake said that planting trees would probably not stop climate change but would certainly slow it, while also cleaning urban air and providing other benefits.

Few people paid attention to Leake's warning about global warming. Instead, people continued to burn fossil fuels. They continued to cut down large areas of forest to clear land for farming, ranching, and urban development.

Some forestry businesses did plant stands of trees, but they did so to produce timber, paper, oil, rubber, and other products derived from trees. The goal was to generate income, not to promote a healthy environment for plants and animals nor to fight climate change. While such tree farms did store some carbon, they also did much environmental damage. The trucks and other machinery used at tree farms burned fossil fuels, polluted waterways, and disturbed the soil. To kill insects that can damage trees, farm operators sprayed them with chemical pesticides which polluted the air and water. To harvest exactly the income-generating products they wanted, operators took a monoculture approach. They planted only one type of tree in an area, such as the Monterey pine. A forest with only one kind of tree does not provide a healthy environment for animals, which rely on a diverse network of plants and trees for food, shelter, and safe places to raise their young.

In the late twentieth century, in the face of widespread deforestation and industrial forestry, a few individuals decided to fight the trend. They decided to plant trees—not for profit but to restore healthy forests on Earth. One of them was Japanese botanist Akira Miyawaki. In the 1970s, he began working on afforestation—planting trees in places where trees hadn't grown before. These places included vacant lots and abandoned factories. Miyawaki collected seeds from ancient Japanese forests; germinated, or sprouted, them; and nurtured the seedlings. Then he planted the young trees in dense stands and let nature take over. After perfecting his growing techniques, he led afforestation projects around the world.

Shubhendu Sharma (*facing page*), an Indian industrial engineer, heard Miyawaki give a talk in India. He became hooked on Miyawaki's ideas. He decided to follow the Japanese botanist's example by planting 224 tree and shrub saplings in his home city of Kashipur, India. Sharma quit his job at the Toyota car company to help plant more than thirty-two thousand trees in his city. He then opened a tree-planting business, Afforestt. His company has gone on to plant more than one hundred forests,

containing more than 450,000 trees in total, in more than forty cities in ten countries. The small forests are planted near schools, apartment

At an afforestation project in India, workers plant a miniature forest on the grounds of Kanakakunnu Palace.

buildings, factories, farms, and even zoos. "A forest can be an integral part of our urban existence," said Sharma. Add his numbers to Miyawaki's forty million trees planted in fifteen countries, and the two have changed the world one tree at a time and launched an entirely new way of greening urban centers.

## TREE TIME

In the twenty-first century, cities all over the world are changing their landscapes by planting trees and urban forests. The city of Darwin, Australia, for example, planted more than 12,500 trees in the late 2010s and early 2020s. The mayor of the city, Kon Vatskalis, aims to establish "a resilient urban forest with cyclone [hurricane] resistant tree species." Milan is working hard to increase its tree numbers. It strives to plant 3 million trees by 2030—one for each resident. By the end of 2021, the city had already planted 9,000 trees.

New York City is another leader in urban greening. Nearly seven hundred thousand trees grow along its streets. The city encourages residents and visitors to learn about and interact with the trees in their neighborhoods. For instance, the city parks department hosts a website with a map of the trees lining city streets. The site includes a form for reporting problems with specific trees—such as unhealthy or injured trees—and information on tree-related community and volunteer events. Visitors to the website can use the map to explore tree species at the citywide, neighborhood, and street levels. Along with information on specific tree species, the site lists the benefits that trees provide to the city, such as the amount of rainwater they intercept, the amount of carbon dioxide they absorb, and the amount of pollution they take from the air (1,259,991 pounds, or 571,522 kg, each year). The website also explains how trees benefit city dwellers by providing cooling and shade, reducing summertime heat, and decreasing wind speeds.

## GREENING UPWARD

In the twenty-first century, architects, urban foresters, and others began to take urban greening to new heights—literally. They began to create vertical forests and other green buildings. Creating vertical forests not only increases the number of trees planted in a city, but it also provides much more tree-planting real estate. Just as many more people can live in a twenty-story apartment building than can live in a one-story building, many more trees can live on a twenty-story building than can live on a single block of land on the ground.

With Bosco Verticale, Boeri inspired other architects to build vertical forests. One of them, in Sydney, Australia, is One Central Park, an apartment tower designed by architect Jean Nouvel and vertical garden pioneer Patrick Blanc. The tower is covered in nearly forty thousand plants. The architects describe the building as "a flower for each resident, and a bouquet for the city." A similar tower is planned for Brisbane, Australia.

## A Green Building Pioneer

American Frank Lloyd Wright played a major role in twentieth-century architecture. He designed more than one thousand structures, including the famous Fallingwater. Designed in 1935, this Pennsylvania home sits in harmony with the site's natural elements. For instance, it contains patios jutting out over a 30-foot (9 m) waterfall. Wright believed that "the mission of an architect is to help people understand how to make life more beautiful, the world a better one for living in, and to give reason, rhyme, and meaning to life."

He also felt that a building should rise out of its natural surroundings. "I go to nature every day for inspiration in the day's work. I follow in building the principles which nature has used in its domain," he explained. He also wrote, "Study nature, love nature, stay close to nature. It will never fail you."

Singapore, a city-state in Southeast Asia, has eighteen "Supertrees"—164-foot (50 m) concrete towers covered with a total of 158,000 plants. Built along the city's Marina Bay, the trees are a magnet for tourists, especially when they are lit up at night. Like live trees, these structures provide shade, filter rainwater, and absorb carbon dioxide and pollution from the air. Park Nova, a vertical forest with fifty-four residences, is scheduled to open in Singapore in 2023.

Mana Foresta is India's first treescraper. It is home to close to four thousand plants and fifty-six human households near bustling Bangalore. This city is the tech hub of India, making it a great place for this innovative project.

Boeri is cheered by the green building revolution. In a manifesto, a statement explaining his views, he says that trees have the power to address many of the world's challenges. They absorb fossil fuel emissions, reduce air pollution, and "improve the quality of health and life in a city." The manifesto explains, "Increasing forests and trees in the world's cities can help absorb $CO_2$ [carbon dioxide], drastically reduce pollution, energy consumption and the 'urban heat island' effect." It also says that urban forests "make cities safer, more pleasant, healthier and attractive." Finally, the manifesto urges, "We have the duty to launch a global campaign on urban forestry in order to multiply the presence of forests and trees in our cities."

Trees grow on the roof and through the windows of Hundertwasser House in Vienna, Austria. Built in the 1980s, the house was designed by Friedensreich Hundertwasser.

# CHAPTER 3

# A Vertical Forest

# Takes Root

**Stefano Boeri is obsessed with trees**—a fascination that began in childhood. "Every tree is a character in the life-giving story of the planet," he says.

Boeri was born in 1956 in Milan. As a boy, he loved the book *Il Barone Rampante* (Baron in the Trees) by Italo Calvino. It tells of a twelve-year-old boy, Cosimo Piovasco di Rondò, who leaves the ground one evening in 1767 to live in the trees for the rest of his life. Boeri's mother, Cini Boeri, was a well-known interior designer and architect. He remembers romping among birch trees at the building site of a house his mother designed in the woods near Italy's Lake Maggiore.

## GROWING A GREEN ARCHITECT

When Boeri was sixteen, Austrian artist and architect Friedensreich Regentag Dunkelbunt Hundertwasser visited Milan. He championed environmental protection and used performance art to promote his ideas. In one case, Hundertwasser stood near Milan's famous La Scala Opera House with a small oak tree in his hand, advocating for incorporating trees in the design of houses and courtyards.

In March 1971, while living in the Giudecca neighborhood of Venice, Italy, Hundertwasser wrote an essay called "Forestation of the City." Giudecca had lots of old palaces with gardens, but it was also filled with shipyards and factories. The artist said that humans were harming Earth by destroying nature and that people needed to fight on nature's behalf. "We are in a state of war. The roofs must turn into green forests, as well as the roads," he wrote.

Hundertwasser believed it might take a thousand years to repair the damage humans had done to Earth, but that shouldn't dissuade us from acting, he said. He urged people to start immediately. In a project in September 1973, Hundertwasser blocked off a street in Milan and, using a big crane, had fifteen trees placed inside several apartment buildings. The day after the installation, Milan's residents saw branches poking out from the windows of the buildings.

Boeri was still a teenager then. The environmental movement was gathering strength all around him. For instance, in 1972 the song "L'albero di 30 piani" ("A Thirty-Story Tree") played on the radio in Italy. Written by Adriano Celentano, the song focused on pollution-filled cities. It spoke of factories that colored the air with black smoke. But it also talked of "something growing . . . maybe it's a tree, yes a tree of thirty floors."

Boeri graduated from the university Politecnico di Milano with a degree in architecture in 1980. Nine years later, he received his PhD from the Istituto Universitario di Architettura di Venezia and became a professor of urban planning at Politecnico di Milano. Guest professorships, or short-term teaching jobs, at other universities took him to cities around the world, including Moscow and Boston.

In the first decade of the twenty-first century, Stefano Boeri began to visualize green buildings and green cities. This artwork shows his vision for Milan's Green River.

In 2007, while on a business trip in the desert city of Dubai in the United Arab Emirates, Boeri found himself looking out at the city's modern skyscrapers. Each of those buildings, clad in ceramic, metal, and glass, was reflecting sunlight and generating heat. That's when Boeri had an aha moment. "It occurred to me to create two eco-friendly towers covered not in glass but in leaves—leaves of plants, shrubs, but especially the leaves of trees," he wrote.

## The Rise of Environmentalism

The modern environmental movement emerged in the late twentieth century, but environmentalism has deep roots. The 1231 Constitutions of Melfi published in Sicily banned the burning of toxic substances to limit pollution. The English king Edward I limited coal burning in London in 1306 because of the smog, or air pollution, it created. But coal burning continued in London and elsewhere. In the seventeenth century, John Evelyn, a British naturalist and gardener, compared polluted London to "the suburbs of Hell."

Fast-forward to 1952, when killer smog filled the air of London with sulfur dioxide, carbon dioxide, and smoke. A mix of industrial pollution and fog, the smog reduced visibility to only 3 feet (0.9 m) and darkened the sky for days. The Great Smog of 1952 sickened thousands of people. Some people who were already ill with respiratory diseases died from the smog. Four years later, to prevent such disasters, the British Parliament passed the nation's first Clean Air Act. The law placed restrictions on coal burning and other air-polluting practices.

Across the ocean, Henry David Thoreau wrote about his famous Walden Pond in 1852. Naturalist John Muir founded the Sierra Club in 1892. They, along with others writing about the natural world, spearheaded the green movement in the United States. In his 1949 book *A Sand County Almanac*,

Scottish immigrant John Muir led the movement to conserve vast areas of American wilderness.

American naturalist Aldo Leopold included an essay called "Land Ethic." It focused on the relationship between people and the land and stressed that humans, wildlife, soil, and water were all part of one community. American biologist and writer Rachel Carson published her best-selling book *Silent Spring* in the early 1960s. In it, Carson moved away from the trend of celebrating nature to decry the use of agricultural pesticides, which were killing fish, birds, and other wildlife. The book stirred public awareness and led to the banning of the pesticide DDT.

The year 1970 was a turning point in the US environmental movement. That year President Richard Nixon and the US Congress established the Environmental Protection Agency, charged with protecting the environment from pollution. Following that, Congress passed the Clean Water Act, the Clean Air Act, and other environmental laws. Americans observed Earth Day for the first time in 1970. It became an annual event, celebrating the world's environmental treasures and calling for their protection.

Jumping ahead a few decades, Greta Thunberg, a Swedish teenager, took the lead in the fight to combat climate change in 2018. She urged world leaders to commit to reducing carbon emissions quickly and dramatically to save Earth from a climate disaster. She also inspired many other young people to join the environmental movement.

Greta Thunberg speaks at a rally to fight climate change in Washington, DC.

## Become an Architect

An architect's job is to plan, design, and oversee the construction or redesign of a building. Some architects work solely on renovation projects, while others design new structures. Buildings can range from houses to skyscrapers to shopping centers. Many architects specialize in commercial, residential, or industrial buildings. Others are specialists in interior design, renovating old structures, conservation, or building in cities. As with many other professions, becoming an architect takes time and study. The job combines creativity with mathematics and science. Additionally, architects must be great communicators so that they can successfully present their projects and explain their designs to many people, including builders, electricians, and clients. Working with urban planners, architects make a difference in our landscape, our lives, and the way we live. The buildings they create usually outlive many generations.

## FROM INSPIRATION TO DESIGN

One of Boeri's clients, an American real estate company, wanted to build an apartment complex in Milan. Thinking about his inspiration in Dubai, Boeri starting drawing plans for two tree-covered apartment towers. Would the clients agree to such a radical design? Could he move his idea from the page to the bustling city of Milan? Architects often design projects that are never built. Would this be one of them?

Boeri gave a picture of his two towers to a journalist. It appeared in an Italian newspaper with the title "The First Ecological and Sustainable Tower Is Going to Be Created in Milan." The article accompanying the picture highlighted the benefits of the plan, including that the leaves on the building's trees would absorb carbon dioxide and pollution from Milan's air, while also releasing oxygen into the air.

The buildings would be extraordinary. Many apartment buildings have balconies where residents grow plants. But these aren't built into the architecture of the building; they are additions. Boeri's towers would have giant balconies with enough room and strength to hold entire trees. The trees would range in height from about 9 to 30 feet (3 to 9 m). There would be two trees, eight shrubs, and forty bushes for every one building resident. "Effectively, it was the idea of building a Tower for trees—which incidentally housed human beings," Boeri said. He compared each building to "one big tree, where the balconies are the branches, all the plant species are the leaves, the central body of the building is the trunk and the roots are water supply systems."

Many questions remained. Could the building and the balconies support the weight of so many trees? Would the trees survive strong winds on the buildings' upper floors? How would all the plants be watered and maintained? Would tree and plant roots damage the building's structure? Even without all the answers, Boeri's client let the building design go forward.

Bosco Verticale is a green oasis in the busy Porto Nueva district of Milan.

# CHAPTER 4

# Building a Treescraper

Stefano Boeri didn't have all the answers to the questions about treescrapers, but he knew where to find them. He gathered a team of engineers, soil scientists, botanists, builders, and fellow architects to work on each of these challenges. The plan called for two residential towers: one with nineteen floors, the other with twenty-seven. The towers would have almost 500 midsize trees, 250 small ones, five thousand shrubs, and eleven thousand other plants. It would have roughly the same amount of trees and plants as a 2.5-acre (1 ha) forest.

Boeri brought Italian agronomist (soil and crop expert) Laura Gatti onto the team, along with landscape artist and garden manager Emanuela Borio. Together they would work to design the botanical aspect of the project.

Like Boeri, Gatti looked at trees a lot when she was young. She noted how they changed season by season. And like Boeri, the environmental movement in Milan in the 1970s influenced her. After studying agricultural science, she became a professor at the University of Milan, teaching courses on parks and gardens, nurseries, and the management of green spaces in cities. She also worked as a consultant for the US Green Building Council, an organization dedicated to making buildings more environmentally friendly. For the Bosco Verticale project, she would help select the trees and plants. She would also determine the best conditions and maintenance needed to ensure that the trees survived.

## SHOPPING FOR TREES

It took two years of planning to determine the right mixture of plants and trees for Bosco Verticale. The team had to consider many factors beyond just the look of the trees on the tower. Team members wanted to avoid trees that might produce allergic reactions in residents. So they ruled out birch trees. Winds increase with height, so they had to choose trees that could withstand strong winds hitting the buildings' upper stories. They wanted trees that were hardy and that had built-in defenses, such as chemical secretions or waxy coatings on leaves to repel insects. They also looked at what species were the best for trapping dust and pollution. Their selections included "holm oaks, trees belonging to the Parrotia family, Turkish hazelnuts, beeches, maples, plum trees," writes Gatti on her website.

The team then concentrated on the look of the towers. The planners wanted the buildings to be both functional and beautiful. As if painting with plants, Gatti and the team decided on "colorful and showy" evergreen trees for the southwest side. Deciduous trees (whose leaves change color and drop in the fall) would display their "autumn hues" on the northeast side. And plants on the eastern side included "soft, fresh, spring tones."

After they dropped their leaves, the deciduous trees would allow sunlight into building windows in winter, to help warm the interiors of the apartments. In summer, their leaves would provide shade from the strong summer sun.

## ENGINEERING THE DESIGN

The selected plants and trees couldn't be planted on ordinary balconies in traditional, freestanding pots. They would be too big and heavy for these structures. Instead, the trees needed to be in strong containers embedded into the balconies, with lots of soil and other structural supports. The engineering firm Arup Italy came up with many solutions for strengthening the towers and terraces. The towers were built of strong reinforced concrete. Support beams called cantilevers gave extra strength to the terraces. Individual trees were anchored to the terraces with safety ropes so that if branches or trunks were damaged or broken, the wood would stay in place rather than falling to the ground. Steel cages were placed around the roots of the largest trees to

## Wind Tunnel Testing

How would trees survive in the winds that would whip around Boeri's tall towers in Milan? To find out, the team tested trees at Florida International University's Wall of Wind, a 16,000-square-foot (1,486 sq. m) facility in Miami. Funded by the National Science Foundation, the facility enables researchers from all over the world to test and understand the impact of wind on structures. Its twelve fans can blow simulated winds up to 157 miles (252 km) per hour.

The Bosco Verticale team took real trees to the large facility, where they were exposed to winds up to 122 miles (196 km) per hour. Only trees that withstood the strong winds expected on the towers' upper floors were used in the design.

Creating Bosco Verticale was a challenge for designers, arborists, and builders. Balconies had to be strong enough to support heavy trees. Trees had to be able to withstand strong winds hitting the towers' upper stories.

prevent them from overturning in major windstorms. All the chosen plants, watered with an automatic irrigation system, were tested in a wind tunnel in Florida to make sure they could withstand the stress of high winds on the towers.

Natural soil—the kind people normally use when planting trees—is heavy. If this soil were used to support all the trees on

Bosco Verticale, the building wouldn't be able to handle the weight. The team needed a lighter soil to support and nourish all the trees and plants in the vertical forest. They created a mixture of agricultural soil, decaying plant matter, and lightweight rock. The mixture took up less space than ordinary soil and also weighed less. It would be placed in the strong containers embedded in the buildings' balconies.

All plants need water, and the tower design included an eco-friendly irrigation system. Gray water—water that residents used for daily bathing, dishwashing, and laundry—would run into irrigation pipes to water the plants. Gray water isn't clean enough for humans to drink, but it's safe for nourishing plants.

While trees on the towers would help with cooling by providing shade in summer, residents still needed power for heating and for running home appliances. To provide some of this power, designers included solar panels on the towers' rooftops. They would collect energy from the sun and convert it to electricity.

## A HOME IN THE TREES

Construction of the towers began in 2009 and finished in 2014. After Bosco Verticale opened, it quickly won design awards and got lots of press coverage. And residents moved in and began living in the treescraper. How did they like their new digs?

Simona Pizzi moved into Bosco Verticale when it opened in 2014. In an episode of the TV show *Sustainable*

### By the Numbers: Breathing Building Stats

Scientists have determined that Bosco Verticale's cherry, apple, olive, beech, larch, and other trees absorb roughly 14 tons (13 t) of carbon dioxide and 57 tons (52 t) of pollutants each year while also producing about 9 tons (8 t) of oxygen.

## Flying Gardeners

It takes extraordinary measures to care for a vertical forest. The trees are living on a skyscraper, not growing on the ground. Keeping such trees healthy requires advanced skills. Arborists are specialists in planting and caring for trees. Those working on a vertical forest must have extra skills. They must be "flying gardeners"—brave enough to hang from ropes attached to rooftops and to climb down like a rock climber between balconies to prune branches, clear leaves, and check on the health of trees.

This rendering by Stefano Boeri shows his plan for green buildings and green corridors in Milan.

*Energy*, Pizzi said, "It doesn't feel like we're living right in the middle of busy Milan, where everything goes quite fast." She added, "Having these plants right on the terrace, real trees, has certainly had a positive impact on my life. It brings [the] temperature down in the summer . . . . It's very pleasant."

With the first vertical forest created successfully, Boeri envisioned the "creation of a number of vertical forests in the city." He also hoped to develop a "network of environmental corridors" that would connect various green spaces of the city and provide wildlife with a pathway through the urban environment. He imagined a bird flying from a tree on a green tower to a park, then continuing on to another park or another tower, and so on, all through the city. He envisioned bees and butterflies making this journey too. The network would provide places for wildlife—especially flying or climbing wildlife—to rest and feed. It would make the urban environment richer and healthier for wildlife as well as humans.

# CHAPTER 5

# Wild Cities

**Urban green spaces are crucial for many reasons.** Not only do they provide benefits for human residents but they also provide habitat for all kinds of organisms, from fish and mammals to birds and insects. You might not always see animals in cities, but they are there. From pigeons and peregrine falcons in New York City to mountain lions in Los Angeles to monkeys and leopards in Mumbai cities are filled with wildlife. If you live in a big city, look closely. You might see a falcon or a red-tailed hawk flying above you. You might see a squirrel scurrying in a park. Animals contribute to the energy of cities and provide birdwatchers and other animal lovers with enjoyment. Birds, bees, and other insects carry pollen from flower to flower, helping plants reproduce. They also give people a chance to witness nature in action. Cities that provide exposure to nature and offer opportunities to care for nature are called biophilic cities. These types of cities help improve our physical and mental health.

Although there are many benefits to having animals in our urban places, sometimes animals and people clash. For instance, rats in crowded cities can carry disease and gnaw through wires, insulation, and other materials in buildings. And buildings and traffic can create obstacles and cause wildlife deaths.

The amount of wildlife that an urban area can support depends on the amount of green spaces available. In addition to city parks, animals live in abandoned lots, community gardens, lawns, and the trees lining streets. Vertical forests and green roofs give animals refuge and habitat. "If we create the space, the animals will come," said British naturalist Sir David Attenborough on the TV show *Planet Earth II*.

A peregrine falcon perches on a ledge in a big city. Trees and green buildings make cities more welcoming to birds and other animals.

## THE TOWER HABITAT

The term *biodiversity* means "diverse plant and animal life." In a biodiverse ecosystem, many different kinds of plants and animals all work together for health and survival. For example, plants provide animals with life-giving oxygen. Insects feed on plants, and birds feed on insects. As they travel from flower to flower looking for nectar and other food, birds and insects also help pollinate flowers.

# Bringing the Outdoors In: Biophilia Benefits

The word *biophilia* comes from Greek words meaning "love of life." American biologist E.O. Wilson described biophilia as the human instinct to surround one's self with living organisms. It's a concept embraced by many green infrastructure professionals, including the Bosco Verticale team. "We just need to learn how [the] urban ecosystem works and to become urban gardeners," said Laura Gatti in her 2019 TEDx Talk. Studies have shown that being around nature for even short periods of time can provide many health benefits, both physical and mental. Spending time outdoors can increase productivity, improve mood, and reduce stress. We can extend these benefits by integrating plants and trees into our living spaces.

Integrating biophilia design into your own space is easy. You don't need a large budget or even a lot of space. Living walls, gardens, and green infrastructure are great if you have the means to accommodate them, but also consider adding natural materials, patterns, and furniture into your room decor or even your school locker. It can be as simple as hanging a picture of the outdoors on your wall or, if you have the opportunity, putting a plant or fish tank on your desk. Place a chair near a window for reading, open your curtains to bring in sunlight, or hang a nature-inspired mobile from your ceiling. Play soothing nature sounds before sleep. You can create your very own indoor ecosystem by including natural materials, nature-themed artwork, and plants in your life.

Biodiversity is in decline around the world. Human activities such as building, hunting, logging, and monocultural farming have directly—and indirectly, through climate change—harmed many plant and animal species. Air and water pollution have harmed many others. When one species goes extinct, or dies out completely, the entire ecosystem suffers. For instance, without the bees that normally spread their pollen, a plant species might not be able to reproduce.

Cities can be tough on biodiversity. Vehicles and buildings emit pollution that can sicken plants and animals. Shiny glass windows are hazardous for migrating birds. Roads and freeways are barriers that divide and harm wildlife. Cars and trucks often hit and kill animals that attempt to cross freeways. And roadways carve up ecosystems, making it difficult for animals to find mates or places to raise their young. But that doesn't have to be. City parks and other green spaces can be biodiverse habitats—so can vertical forests like Bosco Verticale.

Bosco Verticale is in the Porta Nuova area of Milan, a bustling place with shopping and a train station. But even in this urban setting, the towers support a balanced ecosystem. Wildlife is abundant here. "The extraordinary thing that we did not expect was the incredible amount of birds that nested here," Boeri said in 2017. "We have small hawks on the roofs, and swifts that had previously disappeared from Milan." By 2018 more than twenty species of birds, including common blackbirds, redstarts, wood pigeons, Eurasian blackcaps, kestrels, hooded crows, Italian sparrows, pale swifts, and martins, were nesting in Bosco Verticale.

## Biodiversity by the Numbers

Bosco Verticale is a biodiverse ecosystem. It is home to 480 human beings, 711 trees, sixteen hundred birds and insects, five thousand shrubs, and fifteen thousand other plants.

# New York's High Line

High above the streets of New York City, winding around office and apartment buildings, is the High Line, a public park unlike most others. It's built along an old railway line, on top of an elevated structure used for train traffic from 1934 to 1980. The High Line opened to the public in 2009. It's an example of how leftover city spaces can be transformed, providing humans with natural connections.

The 1.5-mile (2.4 km) greenway is popular with workers on lunch break, tourists visiting New York, and joggers. About 7.6 million people visited the park in 2015. It is home to lots of wildlife, including three bat species, two hundred bird species, and more than three hundred flowering plants. The park's many bees pollinate the plants, helping them reproduce. Human beekeepers help the bees by building and maintaining artificial beehives, where the bees raise their young and produce honey. People can even buy honey from the beehives at the park.

New York's High Line Park is built on top of an old railway line.

## Squirrel Friends

Cities are full of squirrels. This is largely because nineteenth-century park designers welcomed squirrels in urban park landscapes. They agreed with American naturalist John Burroughs, who wrote in 1900 that the squirrel was "an elegant creature" that "excites feelings of admiration akin to those awakened by the birds and the fairer forms of nature." Park managers captured squirrels in rural woodlands and brought them to parks in Philadelphia, Boston, New York City, and other cities. The animals made their nests in trees, which also provided nuts for their food. In New York's Central Park, many visitors fed peanuts to the squirrels. Squirrel numbers grew as the animals reproduced.

By 1883 more than fifteen hundred squirrels were living in Central Park. They continue to thrive there. In 2019 more than three hundred volunteers set out to count the park's squirrels. They made two counts—one in the morning and another at night. Altogether, the volunteers made about three thousand squirrel sightings. But because some squirrels were likely spotted by more than one volunteer and counted more than once, the team's final calculation was lower. It determined that about twenty-three hundred squirrels were living in the park. These squirrels provide many opportunities for people to observe and enjoy nature. At the same time, they provide a service to the environment by dispersing seeds that help keep cities green into the future.

A 2018 scientific study published in the *Journal of Urban Ecology* compared numbers of birds at green buildings like Bosco Verticale with those at ordinary buildings. The study found that green buildings had about two to five times more birds than the other buildings. And these birds weren't just stopping by the trees to rest and look for food. They were building nests and having babies there.

# The Importance of City-Dwelling Pollinators

Insect pollinators, such as bees, have suffered from significant population declines in many parts of the world. These species play an important role in preserving our global biodiversity and sustaining our food supply and natural resources. Population declines happen everywhere, but a study published in *Conservation Biology* showed that populations of wild bees continue to survive in cities where harmful agricultural pesticides and herbicides are not used. American cities with this pollinator-friendly practice include Chicago, Phoenix, and New York City. This green practice is also found in cities around the world, including Berlin, Germany, and Melbourne, Australia. Green spaces in cities help support healthy ecosystems and biodiversity by providing access to plants and nectar for these pollinators.

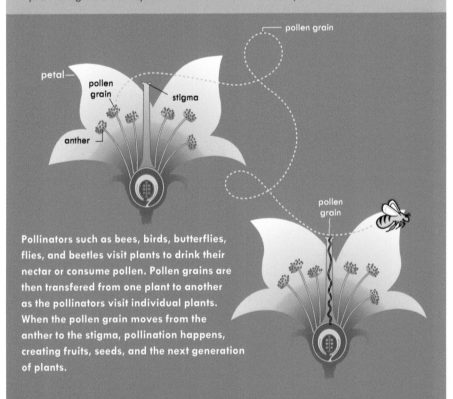

Pollinators such as bees, birds, butterflies, flies, and beetles visit plants to drink their nectar or consume pollen. Pollen grains are then transfered from one plant to another as the pollinators visit individual plants. When the pollen grain moves from the anther to the stigma, pollination happens, creating fruits, seeds, and the next generation of plants.

Bosco Verticale also hosts several insect species, including bumblebees, hermit wild bees, butterflies, and hoverflies. Some insects that live in the vertical forest are harmful. For instance, aphids can damage or destroy the plants and trees there. Instead of using harmful chemicals to kill these pests, scientists at Bosco Verticale took a natural approach. On May 29, 2014, they released 1,250 ladybird beetles (*Adalia bipunctata*) onto the tower's terraces. The beetles prey on the aphids, keep their numbers down, and help keep the plants healthy.

Bosco Verticale is a jewel in Milan's urban greening necklace. The city intends to make itself even greener by planting three million trees by 2030. They'll show up on flat rooftops and school courtyards as well as along city streets. The plan also includes turning an old, unused railway network into seven parks, with twenty-five trees planted in the parks each year. All these trees will provide more habitat for wildlife in addition to all the benefits they provide to humans.

The Dakpark ("roof park") sits on top of a shopping mall in Rotterdam, the Netherlands.

# CHAPTER 6

# Green Roofs

Have you ever seen the roof of a bus stop or other structure—maybe even your school—covered in a thick carpet of growing green plants? If so, you sighted a green roof, also called an ecoroof, living roof, or roofscape. Look up as you walk around your town or city and see how many you can spot. You might even spot one on top of a city bus! Like other urban greening ideas, green roofs aren't new, but they are becoming more popular because they can do much for us and the health of our planet.

Green roofs provide the same benefits as treescrapers and other green structures. They provide shade, filter pollution from the air, and offer homes for birds, insects, and other animals. Green roofs also help keep buildings (and buses) cool by removing heat from the air. This happens through transpiration and evaporation. During transpiration, plants release water through their leaves. Evaporation is when that water changes from liquid into gas—water vapor. The energy that fuels evaporation is heat. When water evaporates from a green roof, water vapor pulls heat away from the roof, leaving it cooler than before. This helps lower the temperature of the building beneath a green roof and cools the surrounding area, a benefit in urban heat islands.

## ANCIENT ROOTS

The first green roofs were probably built thousands of years ago. The Hanging Gardens of Babylon, built on the rooftops and terraces of a big brick building in land that became a part of Iraq, were planted around 500 BCE. Ancient writers called them one of the Seven Wonders of the World. Although archaeologists and historians haven't pinpointed the garden's exact location, they think the gardeners grew the plants not to produce food but for the pleasure of Babylonian rulers.

People in Scandinavia (the modern European nations of Norway, Sweden, and Denmark) have been using green roofs for hundreds of years. In the Middle Ages (about 500 to 1500 CE) and perhaps earlier, Scandinavians covered their homes with turf (sod)—a thick mat of soil bound together by grasses and plant roots. The thick living layer served as insulation, preventing the passage of heat. This kept in warmth from fireplaces in winter and helped block out heat from the sun in summer. Turf roofs called *torvtak* were common in rural Norway until the eighteenth century. They are still used in many places. The turf covered the roofs of log cabins and was placed over layers of birch bark. It was a good insulator, and it kept rain from seeping through roofs.

People also built sod homes in the Arctic—regions near the North Pole. In past centuries, the Inuit people built sod igloos in summer. We typically think of igloos as being made of ice and snow, but these dome-shaped houses can be made from sod or stone too. Farther south, on the American Great Plains nineteenth-century settlers sometimes built whole houses out of blocks of sod.

Sod-covered roofs were common in Norway in earlier centuries. They helped insulate houses and also absorbed rainwater.

## GREEN ROOF REVOLUTION

The modern green roof movement began in Germany in the 1960s. That's when botanist and university researcher Reinhard Bornkamm wrote about German buildings with plants growing on top. The buildings, constructed around 1900, hadn't been originally made with green roofs. But over the years, plants had naturally started growing on the mixture of gravel and sand on the rooftops. In 1969 builders created GENO-Haus, a thirteen-story bank building with a green roof in Stuttgart, Germany. Munich, another German city, has required green roofs on all new buildings since 1996.

Generally, green roofs are intensive or extensive. The two differ in weight, the amount of water they can absorb, and the variety of plantings involved. Intensive green roofs have a thick layer of soil, usually between 6 and 12 inches (15 to 30 cm). This deep layer can support a variety of plants, even some trees. Extensive roofs have a

After nearly 500 birds were killed by crashing into New York City's Jacob K. Javits Convention Center in a period of four years, new laws were put in place that included bird-friendly panels. City greening has also helped. The recently installed seven-acre green roof is a haven for birds that also absorbs seven million gallons of storm water runoff annually and contributes to the reduction of energy consumption by the Center.

thinner layer of soil, usually 6 inches deep or less, which can support only grasses or ground cover plants. Because intensive roofs are thicker, they can also absorb more rainwater than extensive roofs.

A green roof's ability to absorb heavy rains is beneficial in places that are prone to flooding. Green roofs are part of a plan to turn the Chinese cities of Wuhan and Chongqing into "sponge cities" to combat heavy floods. The plan also includes plants growing on building walls and pavement that is porous, or filled with tiny openings. These openings will allow water to seep into the ground instead of flooding roadways. Combined, all these features will reduce the amount of rainwater that flows onto city streets and rushes into sewers.

Dutch architect and green infrastructure specialist Denise Houx explains that green roofs must be combined with additional technology to be effective. She says it isn't enough just to put dirt on a roof and grow plants. Green roofs must have equipment to monitor water levels and to channel excess water off the roof when needed. According to

Houx, a well-designed roof "means more cooling and an increase in air quality." If designers go one step further, Houx says, they can make green roofs more eco-friendly by installing solar panels above the plants.

While the United States hasn't fully embraced green roofs, Europe has. There, laws and governments' financial support move many projects forward. In 2021 the Italian government said that if a homeowner wanted to make their house greener and more energy-efficient, the government would pay the cost and even a little extra. One of the leading countries in the urban greening movement is the Netherlands, where green roofs have been installed on everything from bus stops to housetops. Rotterdam in the Netherlands is on target to have eight hundred thousand green roofs planted by 2030.

Some American cities are working to increase their ecoroof numbers. The city council in Portland, Oregon, adopted the Central City 2035 plan. It requires green roofs atop buildings of 20,000 square feet (1,858 sq. m) or more in commercial zones within Portland's city center. A study from Portland's Reed College identified close to four hundred ecoroofs in the city in 2019, totaling nearly 1.4 million square feet (130,064 sq. m), the size of about four football fields.

## By the Numbers: Green Jobs

American Rivers, a US conservation organization, says that a $10 billion investment to build 50 billion square feet (4.7 billion sq. m) of green roofs in the United States would benefit the economy. It would create almost two hundred thousand jobs—for roof installers, botanists, horticulturists, landscapers, and maintenance people. But an area of 50 billion square feet equals only about 1 percent of all the roofs in the country. If the United States is going to embrace green roofs and their benefits, it needs a much larger investment and a qualified workforce to match. Look for more green roof job opportunities in the future.

These ecoroofs feature many shade-tolerant and drought-resistant plants. The ability to tolerate shade is important because most of the year, Portland is rainy and cloudy. Because of climate change, Portland's geographic region, called the Pacific Northwest, also has increasingly dry, hot summers, so plants must be tolerant of this weather too. Most ecoroofs in Portland are intensive roofs with deep soil and a variety of plants.

## ROOFTOP COMMUNITIES

Green roofs pose many challenges for their designers. For roofs atop tall buildings, designers must choose plants that can withstand strong winds. Studies such as those conducted in Florida for Bosco Verticale have helped botanists determine which plants do best in high winds and atop tall buildings. Botanists also know that lower green roofs are better at attracting birds and insects than higher ones. It's easier for animals to reach the top of low-rise buildings, which have less wind and easier access to the ground, than to reach the tops of high-rises.

Because of their accessibility, many low-rise green rooftops have blossomed into biodiverse habitats. One 2012 study in London found that bats regularly visited green roofs on low-rise buildings to munch on insects living there—benefiting plants by eating insects that might harm them. According to Kwantlen Polytechnic University plant ecologist Christine Thuring, the green roof sitting atop the Vancouver Convention Centre in British Columbia is frequently visited by insect pollinators. The roof, established in 2009, is home to four hundred thousand plants, including flowers that attract bees and butterflies. Other insect residents include spiders and beetles. And the many insects, in turn, attract hungry songbirds. Biodiversity also includes animals that are primarily plant-eaters: Thuring has even spotted a goose nesting on the convention center roof.

Green roofs also provide homes for threatened and endangered animals. The numbers of these animals have dwindled because of habitat destruction, hunting, climate change, pollution, and other human-made dangers. Some of these animals are at risk of going extinct. Examples include the northern lapwing (*Vanellus vanellus*), an endangered wader bird native to Eurasia that has suffered from habitat loss. The northern lapwing naturally lives in low growing or grazed plant communities, such as wet meadows. In many areas, like Switzerland, this habitat is often drained for farming, causing the birds to lose their breeding spots and their numbers to decline. Due to the growth of agriculture and urban sprawl the bird has now become a vulnerable and high priority species in Europe. Green roofs might help save these birds from extinction. Observers have noted northern lapwing living on nine green roofs in Switzerland between 2005 and 2010, particularly roofs with low growing plants saw an increase of chicks. Perhaps these roofs will help northern lapwings and other species increase in numbers.

In Zurich, Switzerland, green roofs have helped a rare and endangered wall lizard. The city has many living roofs on top of platforms at railway

Calhoun School in New York City has a green roof with lawns and gardens.

stations. In some places, roof designers created towers and passageways out of stones and vines. They look like the dry riverbed habitat the lizards naturally prefer, and lizards are making their homes there. Naturalists hope that these roofs will help the lizards increase in numbers.

Another green roof in Switzerland is also helping endangered species. This roof covers a water treatment plant near Zurich. The building dates to 1914. Its original roof was made of soil from a prairie near the construction site. Over the years, the seeds of prairie plants started to grow in the rooftop soil. The roof developed into a wet prairie ecosystem with 175 plant species. Many of those plants are no longer in other parts of the city. They died out elsewhere but thrived in the prairie soil on top of the water plant. Among the rare plants living on the roof are nine species of orchids.

## A RARE DISCOVERY

Ecologist Mark Patterson, who manages the garden on top of the Nomura International bank building in London, was surprised to discover rare orchids growing there in 2021. A colony of these orchids, members of the species *Serapias parviflora*, had died out a few years before. People thought the orchids were gone from England for good. But here they were again on the green roof in London. How did they get there?

*Serapias parviflora*, a small purple orchid, is native to land around the Mediterranean Sea and to the Atlantic coast of France, Portugal, and Spain. Patterson thinks seeds from the orchids traveled with the wind from the European mainland to the bank's green roof. "The plants could have originated on the continent [mainland Europe] and been brought over the [English] Channel on southerly winds," said Patterson. "Once settled on the Nomura roof, the seeds would have [gotten nutrients from fungus] enabling them to germinate and grow." He added that the chances of this happening were tiny. Yet the plants grew. The roof has fifteen orchid plants, growing among 159 other plant species. It is also home to seventeen bee species and a host of other wildlife.

# Past to Present

People build gardens for many reasons—to grow food, to attract
birds and other wildlife, or to relax amid the plants and flowers there.
Sometimes people create botanical gardens, designed for the growth
and study of specific kinds of plants. For example, in 1545 leaders at
the University of Padua in Italy built a garden for the growth and study
of medical plants—plants used to heal sicknesses. The garden still
operates in Padua although it has grown much larger, with many more
types of plants added over the years. Modern-day visitors can see
the early garden design, including a historic palm tree planted there
in 1585. Visitors can also see new highlights, such as the impressive
Solar Active Building, a greenhouse with solar panels. The building
marks the entrance to the site's Biodiversity Garden, home to about
thirteen hundred species of plants.

## CELEBRATING GREEN ROOFS

On June 6, 2021, a group called Livingroofs.org and the European Federation of Green Roofs and Walls held the first World Green Roof Day—a celebration of green roofs and their benefits. On that day, Twitter was filled with stories of green roofs, all posted using the hashtag #WGRD2021. Celebrants also posted pictures of beautiful green roofs and their innovative technology. The photos showed everything from backyard sheds to major projects like Chicago's award-winning Studio Gang Rooftop Prairie. In one growing season, this 4,700-square-foot (437 sq. m) wheat field, on the roof of a three-story building downtown, produced enough wheat to make 66 pounds (30 kg) of whole-wheat pastry flour.

Workers harvest wheat at the Studio Gang Rooftop Prairie in Chicago.

A green roof on a bus stop shelter in Flint, Michigan

World Green Roof Day celebrant Spencer Fletcher, a wildlife gardener from the United Kingdom, tweeted about how green roofs promote our connection to nature while supporting wildlife. He wrote, "It's World Green Roof Day, we need to bring nature back in amongst us. Many of us have been disconnected from nature, but we must remember we are part of nature. If we feel part of something we are more likely to want to protect it."

Patrick Blanc created this living wall called L'Oasis d'Aboukir in Paris, France.

# CHAPTER 7

# Living Walls

Bosco Verticale's extraordinary architecture doesn't end with what you can see from the ground. Lots of plants are inside the towers, including on interior walls. And just a few blocks away in Milan is another green building, Klima Hotel Milano Fiere. Outside, the sixteen-story hotel has a living wall, also called a vertical garden. It is covered with ivy, held in place by a network of wire mesh. Inside, the hotel lobby has more living walls. Designed by the firm Verde Profilo, the hotel offers a relaxing atmosphere inside and makes a bold impression outside with its dramatic green wall.

It might be strange to see a wall of greenery on the side of a city building, inside a hotel or airport, or on the side of a bridge, but living walls are becoming more and more common in cities throughout the world. Inside buildings, green walls transform spaces for living and working. Both inside and out, they offer the same benefits of green roofs and other living architecture. They provide shade and cooling. The plants of a living wall release moisture through transpiration. This is a plus in dry areas. The plants also act as insulation, helping keep buildings cool in hot weather and warm in cold weather. They also block out noise pollution.

Outdoor living walls support not only plants but also a variety of birds and insects. That makes living walls a great way to introduce wildlife into urban areas, where safe animal habitats can be hard to find. Many observers have seen robins, finches, thrushes, and other birds building their nests in living walls. The team at ANS Global in the United Kingdom, a leading designer of green roofs and living walls, reported spotting a nesting pair of common blackbirds in the living wall of their plant nursery.

## A LIVING WALL ARTIST

The biggest name in living walls is French botanist Patrick Blanc, who calls his creations *murs végétal*, or "garden walls." Blanc draws his inspiration from nature—from plants that normally cling to rocks and trees as they grow, such as mosses, ivies, ferns, orchids, and vines. His designs have transformed more than three hundred buildings across the globe, both inside and out, from Bangkok, Thailand, to New York City.

Many of his walls are inside private homes and offices, but others are in public places. One is a wall that Blanc created for the 2021 Orchid Show at the New York Botanical Garden. Another is at the Drew School, a private high school in San Francisco, California. There, two side-by-side living walls cover one face of the building. Travelers can also find Blanc's creations at the Qantas lounges in Sydney and Melbourne, Australia, and at many hotels around the world.

Blanc has become a sort of garden rock star. He sometimes even looks the part, with green-dyed hair and green-painted fingernails.

Patrick Blanc tends to a living wall at the Musée du quai Branly - Jacque Chirac in Paris.

He's a jet-setter who searches for rare plant species in remote jungles, but he is careful not to remove too many plants or to harm the ecosystems he visits. He has even discovered previously unnamed species, such as *Begonia blancii*, which he found growing in the Philippines. Scientists named this species after Blanc.

Blanc's Rainforest Chandelier, hanging in a mall in Bangkok, is an extraordinary work of art. The spiral-shaped green sculpture, covered in ferns and other tropical plants, showcases the rich and diverse plant life of the area. Many of Thailand's rain forests have been cut down to make way for farms and buildings. Blanc's work is a statement about the importance of preserving the remaining forests. Another wall made by Blanc is at the CaixaForum cultural center in Madrid, Spain. The wall covers nearly 5,000 square feet (465 sq. m) and holds more than fifteen thousand plants of 250 different species.

## SCIENTIST FIRST, THEN ARTIST

How did Blanc decide to create art with plants? Like Boeri and Gatti, his fascination with nature began in childhood. He was first drawn to fish inside aquariums and then to the plants in the aquarium ecosystem. As a youngster in Paris, he visited Bois de Boulogne, a large park, every week with his mother and enjoyed its streams and waterfalls. He became fascinated with the green moss and ferns growing on the rocks of the waterfalls.

He studied botany in college. During this time, on a trip to Thailand in 1972, he became interested in tropical forests and the plants inhabiting them. "I did stay in Khao Yai National Park and I did look at all the plants growing out of the soil: on tree trunks and branches, on the rocks in the forest understory, on the cliffs," he remembers. In 1994 his botany work turned to art with his exhibition of vertical gardens at the International Garden Festival in Chaumont-sur-Loire in France. He has been creating art with plants ever since.

As a botanist, Blanc knows how to select plant species that are best suited to each location. Since the lower parts of walls tend to be shady, he places plants there that grow well in shade. For higher sections of walls, he chooses plants that need more sunlight and that grow well at higher elevations. He also designs his walls to echo the biodiversity found in nature. During an event with Stefano Boeri at the World Forum he explained that if "you have simply one ivy . . . it's not like nature," where many species grow together. He aims to include a high diversity of plant species on each wall, which creates more stability in the vertical garden.

In Blanc's creations, the plants don't grow directly on building walls, since this might damage the walls. Instead, he covers walls with a metal framework, lined with two layers of artificial felt. The plants sink their roots into and cling to the felt as they grow. In some designs, Blanc includes pockets of soil for the plants. Plants need water, of course, so Blanc builds irrigation systems into the structures.

## FOUR TYPES OF LIVING WALLS

Living walls are either freestanding, intensive, semi-intensive, or extensive. An ivy-covered building is an extensive green wall. Many types of ivy naturally climb up walls, clinging to bricks and other wall surfaces with their twining stems, roots, and tendrils. For the gardener, little maintenance or cost is involved with an ivy-covered wall. Nature does most of the work, keeping plants alive with natural rainfall and sunlight.

Not only are they low maintenance, but ivy-covered walls can be surprisingly effective in reducing the heat of buildings. Portland State University climate scientist Vivek Shandas measured this ability during a heat wave that hit the Pacific Northwest in the summer of 2021. He explained, "I actually just went around Portland [Oregon] and took a bunch of pictures with my little infrared [heat-measuring] camera. The surface temperature of an ivy-covered wall in an industrial area

Many living walls grow without human help. Here, ivy covers a wall at Princeton University in New Jersey.

was about 119°F [48°C]. Right next to it was a non-ivy-covered wall, which was about 157°F [69°C]—about a 40-degree [20°C] difference in temperature that I could record with my camera."

A semi-intensive wall has a human-made support system covering the wall, such as a trellis or a framework for the plants to cling to as they climb. Intensive green walls have a more complicated support system, with not only a framework but also pockets of soil to hold plant roots and to provide soil nutrients to plants. Freestanding walls look something like hedges. They do not cover building walls but instead stand on their own in the middle courtyards or lobbies. They might be flat living sculptures or green room dividers.

## LIVING WALLS AROUND THE WORLD

Blanc isn't alone in creating living walls. The more you look for them, the more living walls you will see. A living wall inside a lounge in San Francisco International Airport spans two stories. Other airports with interior living walls include O'Hare, Detroit Metropolitan, Miami International, St. Louis Lambert, and more. Many living walls are outdoors, even one with plants in large swirling patterns on the outside of a Saks Fifth Avenue store in downtown Palm Beach, Florida. Designed by SMI Landscape Architecture, this wall covers 840 square feet (78 sq. m) and features 10,920 plants.

In downtown Bogotá, Colombia, a building called Santalaia features the world's largest vertical garden. Designed by the green architecture firm Groncol, the upscale apartment building is covered with more than eighty-five thousand plants. Not only is this garden striking to look at, but it produces enough oxygen to meet the needs of more than thirty-one hundred people every year. Every year it also pulls thousands of pounds of dangerous pollutants and dust from the air.

**Nearly forty thousand plants cover One Central Park in Sydney, Australia.**

At AeroFarms in New Jersey, food plants grow indoors on stacks of trays.

# CHAPTER 8

# Urban Farms

**Imagine a farm that does not take up acres and acres of land.**
Imagine a farm that doesn't have to ship its products many miles
away to consumers. This farm flourishes within a high-rise building,
with food growing on shelves stacked up many stories high. Instead
of sunlight, the plants there get energy from electric lights. Water
comes from an irrigation system instead of rain. The farm supplies
country-fresh produce to city dwellers. It produces tomatoes, lettuce,
and fresh herbs year-round, even during cold winter months. From
the outside, you'd never know that inside the building are hundreds of
racks filled with vegetable plants. They grow without harmful chemical
pesticides, weed killers, or fertilizers. They also grow without rain, soil,
or sunshine. Welcome to an urban farm.

Urban farming is transforming cities into orchards, gardens, and more. From the mom-and-daughter enterprise Brown Girl Eggs (Pittsburgh) to the world's largest urban rooftop farm, Nature Urbaine (Paris), urban farms are thriving. City farms fill empty lots and building rooftops. They are outdoors and indoors. They draw community members to small plots and draw businesspeople to high-tech indoor operations. You might know of a city farm near you, or maybe you've eaten at a restaurant that buys its fruits and vegetables from an urban farm.

## GO GREEN!

Can urban farms help solve pressing global problems? Maybe so. One of these problems is world hunger. Experts say that by the year 2050, the world will have more than nine billion people—and most of them will live in cities. Traditional farms might have a hard time growing enough food for all these people. Urban farms can help fill the gap. They can operate year-round, producing food even in winter, when many traditional farms are unproductive for long stretches. They can also produce food more efficiently than traditional farms, because they take up much less space. For example, at its indoor facility in Newark, New Jersey, AeroFarms produces 2 million pounds (907,185 kg) of produce per year. For a typical outdoor farm to grow that much, it would need almost a hundred times as much land.

Transporting food from rural farms to cities is expensive. This work mostly involves fossil-fuel-burning vehicles, such as trucks and trains, which contribute to climate change. But when farms are right in cities, they can provide food to city residents for much less cost and with less harm to the environment.

Traditional farms pose other environmental hazards. Many large farms spray harmful chemicals on food crops to kill crop-destroying insects, fungi, and weeds. But these chemicals often end up on and inside the crops, so when people eat the food, they also take in small

**Many industrial farms spray dangerous pesticides and herbicides on plants.**

amounts of toxic (poisonous) chemicals. And many traditional farms use chemical fertilizers to help plants grow. During rainstorms, fertilizers, pesticides, and insecticides often wash off farm fields into nearby rivers and lakes, polluting them and harming animals and plants that live in or near the water. Some rural farmers have embraced organic practices instead. They shun chemicals and use eco-friendly methods, such as removing weeds by hand rather than spraying crops with weed killers. Many urban farms use organic methods too. Urban farms that operate indoors also have less need for dangerous chemicals because weed seeds, insects that damage crops, and fungi and bacteria that grow in soil—typical problems for outdoor farms—can't easily get inside indoor farm buildings.

Traditional farms are themselves threatened by climate change. Because of rising temperatures on Earth, more farm areas are prone to drought. Without enough rain, farmers cannot grow the food we all depend on for survival. Climate change is also causing sea levels to rise, sometimes flooding farms and bringing salty water from the ocean to agricultural fields. Crops can't grow in fields flooded with salt water. And climate change is causing more severe storms, which can also flood farm fields. Urban farms offer solutions. With indoor urban operations, farmers can heat or cool buildings as needed to provide the best growing environment for crops. Crops are also protected inside buildings, so farmers don't have to worry about flooding from storms or sea level rise. They also don't have to worry about hail, frost, and other weather hazards that kill crops on outdoor farms.

## PROS AND CONS

When people clear land to plant traditional farms, they often cut down trees, destroy wetlands, and reduce animal habitat. By establishing farms in cities, which are already full of human-made infrastructure, urban farmers don't need to cut down trees or destroy habitat. Urban farms also reduce the amount of energy needed to transport food. This helps preserve ecosystems and biodiversity.

Despite these benefits, urban farming isn't completely environmentally friendly. Plants in indoor urban farms need artificial lighting, and that takes energy, which usually comes from fossil fuels. The lighting inside urban farms also produces heat, so buildings must be cooled with fans and air conditioners, especially during warm summer months. That means more energy usage—and more burning of fossil fuels. But even though indoor urban farming isn't perfect, it still offers advantages over traditional farming. And some urban farms do use innovative, eco-friendly practices. An example is the indoor Tower Farm at O'Hare International Airport. This vertical aeroponic garden produces peppers and lettuce, which are grown year-round for in-airport restaurants, including the famous eateries Tortas Frontera and Wolfgang Puck. The farm recycles wastewater, uses solar panels and wind turbines to create energy, and captures rainwater

Tower Farm is an aeroponic garden inside Chicago's O'Hare Airport that supplies greens for airport restaurants.

for irrigation. This farm and others are moving urban agriculture in a more Earth-friendly direction.

## FARMING TECHNOLOGY

Urban farmers use innovative technology to grow crops inside buildings. One technology is hydroponics. With hydroponics, urban farmers grow plants in nutrient-rich water, without soil. Plant roots still need the physical support that soil normally provides, so hydroponic farmers add peat moss, coconut fibers, or other material that holds the roots in place. Different hydroponic farms use different growing setups. In tall buildings, crops might grow in racks, with stacks reaching to the ceiling. Or plants might be grown on shelves lining the building walls.

Aquaponic farming, a type of hydroponics, involves growing crops and fish together. In an aquaponic system, fish live in a tank of water. Farm operators feed the fish, who expel their waste into the water. The

At an aquaponic farm, fish droppings make the water nutrient-rich. This water then nourishes crops growing in the same system.

nutrient-rich wastewater is pumped to another tank, where food crops grow in the water. The plants absorb nutrients from the pumped-in wastewater, thereby cleaning the water. Then the clean water is pumped back into the fish tank, and the cycle continues. Marianne Cufone runs Growing Local NOLA, an aquaponic farm in New Orleans, Louisiana. There, waste from catfish and koi provides the nutrients needed for her floating trays of herbs, cucumbers, and melons. Crops aren't the only food products that come from aquaponic farms. Many aquaponic farmers raise fish such as tilapia, perch, and bluegill and then sell them to fish markets, restaurants, or food wholesalers.

Other farmers use aeroponic farming. In this variation on hydroponic farming, plants are not rooted in soil or another growing substance. Instead, the plant roots hang below a shelf or inside a tall hollow column, where they are misted with nutrient-rich water.

## SUCCESS STORIES

Ed Harwood of Ithaca, New York, was a pioneer of vertical farming. He started his first indoor farm in an empty canoe factory in Ithaca. In 2004 he launched a farm called GreatVeggies and then founded AeroFarms. Harwood died in 2021, but AeroFarms continues to grow kale, arugula, broccoli, and other veggies inside a 30,000-square-foot (2,787 sq. m) facility in Newark. Located in a former laser tag arena, this vertical aeroponic farm grows plants in racks stacked more than 30 feet (9 m) high. An irrigation system continually mists their roots with water containing nutrients that plants need. Water that drains off the roots is reused, so very little water is wasted. AeroFarms uses nearly 95 percent less water than traditional outdoor farms growing the same kind of plants. Inside the facility, rows and rows of electric lights take the place of natural sunlight. The success of the first AeroFarms led the company to build another inside a former steel supply building.

Urban farms are thriving in other places around the world. Techno Farm Keihanna in Kyoto, Japan, is a big operation. It harvests thirty thousand heads of lettuce a day. Operating since 2018, this vertical farm uses robots to plant seeds, tend seedlings, and harvest produce. A peek inside the farm reveals shelves stacked with tray upon tray of growing lettuces and other green vegetables. Like many vertical farms, this one strives to save water. It recycles 90 percent of the nutrient-rich water used for lettuce cultivation.

## GOING LOW-TECH

Food deserts are places where residents find it hard to buy fresh food. They are often found in inner-city neighborhoods, where many residents are low-income and can't afford fresh, healthy food. And many big US cities lack reliable public transportation, so residents might have no easy way to get to grocery stores that do sell healthy foods. Without access to affordable, healthy food, many city residents eat at fast-food restaurants and buy low-priced processed foods that are

## Nature Urbaine

While many urban farms operate indoors to protect crops from bad weather and pests, some urban farms are outside—even on rooftops. Nature Urbaine, in Paris, is the largest rooftop farm in Europe. The farm, on the roof of a convention center, covers more than 150,000 square feet (13,935 sq. m). Some plants there grow in dirt. Others grow in hydroponic trays. Still other plants grow in small containers on tall aeroponic columns. An irrigation system feeds the plants nutrient-rich water, and no chemical pesticides are used. Nature Urbaine grows produce such as spinach, strawberries, kale, and cabbage. It also grows edible flowers. Paris residents and visitors can pick up farm-fresh produce there on Friday evenings and can even rent their own small plots at the farm to grow produce themselves.

high in starch, sugar, and salt. A long-term diet of such food can lead to diabetes, obesity, and other health problems. Food deserts aren't just an urban problem. In some rural areas, such as the Navajo Nation in the US Southwest, residents don't have easy access to healthy food.

Community gardens can combat food deserts by giving people access to fresh fruits and vegetables grown nearby. In cities large and small, many people have started gardens on vacant city lots. Broadway and movie legend Bette Midler started the New York Restoration Project in 1995. The organization cleans trash out of lots in run-down neighborhoods and gives them new life as community gardens. Fannie's Garden at Paradise on Earth is a New York Restoration Project garden in the Bronx, a borough of New York City. There, thirty-six raised garden beds provide food for neighborhood gardeners.

The garden also serves as an outdoor learning space and play area for students from PS 150, a public elementary school across the street. These students had a hand in designing the garden, and teachers take them there to learn about gardening, plants, and wildlife. The garden also contains picnic tables and hosts outdoor film screenings.

In Miami, Health in the Hood founder Asha Walker says that her organization is making communities healthier one garden at a time. The organization currently runs eight urban farms. Paid staff take care of these eight gardens, but volunteers also pitch in. They help with gardening and fill bags with produce from the garden. Some community members donate garden supplies, and others even donate land for new gardens. Health in the Hood distributes the produce free to needy residents. The gardens also serve as outdoor science classrooms for nearby schools.

The success of community gardens shows that you don't need high-tech equipment, a big building, or a big budget to grow healthy food. All you need is a small patch of land, a dedicated crew, and a commitment to going green.

**Volunteers for Miami's Health in the Hood work in the community garden.**

Liuzhou Forest City is under construction in China. This illustration shows Boeri's design for the finished city.

# CHAPTER 9

# A Green Future

**Aerial photographs are taken from airplanes, balloons, and satellites.** When taken at very high altitudes, aerial photos show large regions of land and water—dark green forests, wide blue seas, and vast brown deserts. When shot from lower levels, the photos show more detail, such as buildings and roads. In most aerial photographs, cities look like cities. You can see grids of streets and lots of darkly colored buildings. You might see a few trees or a park, but mostly you see human-made structures. That view of cities is changing. Around the world, Stefano Boeri and other architects are starting to envision and build entire forest cities. When seen from above, these cities will look nearly all green. You might see a few roadways running through the greenery, or perhaps a lake or river, but green will dominate—there will be treescrapers, green roofs, green parks and plazas, and living walls. The cities will almost look like forests.

One forested city is already under construction. In June 2017, Boeri's design firm, Stefano Boeri Architetti, broke ground on Liuzhou Forest City. The 432-acre (175 ha) development is in the northern part of Liuzhou, a city in southern China. There, Boeri is creating an entire community, with the offices, shops, restaurants, and residences covered with greenery. This forested city will house thirty thousand people, forty thousand trees, and one million other plants. Because of heavy industry, Chinese cities are some of the most polluted places on Earth. Liuzhou Forest City is intended to fight this pollution. The city's trees and plants will absorb an estimated 10,000 tons (9,072 t) of carbon dioxide and 57 tons (52 t) of pollutants a year. The plants and trees will also produce 900 tons (816 t) of oxygen per year.

Liuzhou is just the first forested city. Boeri has designed Smart Forest City Cancún and hopes to build it on Cancún, an island resort in Mexico. He also hopes to build fifteen treescrapers in New York City. If built, the towers will hold as many trees as Central Park does.

## CHALLENGES FROM CRITICS

Some people are skeptical about green architecture. When he first saw the plans for Bosco Verticale, technology writer Tim De Chant said that he doubted the project would ever be built. He said that Boeri's design was unrealistic and that trees would not thrive or even survive at the top of tall buildings. "Life just sucks up there," he wrote, "for you, for me, for trees, and just about everything else except peregrine falcons. It's hot, cold, windy, the rain lashes at you, and the snow and sleet pelt you at high velocity [speed]. Life for city trees is hard enough on the ground. I can't imagine what it's like at 500 feet [152 m], where nearly every climate variable is more extreme than at street level."

## Electric Cars and Urban Greening

Most cars and trucks burn gasoline, a fossil fuel, causing them to emit carbon dioxide and pollutants through their exhaust pipes. According to the US Environmental Protection Agency, a typical passenger car emits about 5.1 tons (4.6 t) of carbon dioxide a year. Multiply this by the estimated 1.5 billion cars used all around the world, and it's clear that cars are a major contributor to climate change. If we want to slow climate change and make our air cleaner, it helps to drive less, use public transportation instead of private cars, and choose vehicles that use cleaner types of fuel. One cleaner option is electric cars. Because they run on electric batteries, electric cars don't emit pollutants when they operate. Generating electricity to charge the cars does add pollution to the air, but far less than the amount released by gasoline-powered cars.

Can electric cars and vertical forests work together to make cities healthier? Boeri and the Fiat car company's Olivier François think they can. "I believe that we are really both promoting the same thing—clear air and healthier cities," said Boeri. François said that Fiat is developing La Prima, an electric version of its popular Fiat 500 automobile. Cleaner cars in combination with vertical forests and other urban greening will create a better future for our cities. For his part, Boeri is designing green buildings with charging stations for electric cars.

Electric cars are an alternative to gasoline-powered cars.

Boeri addressed such criticism at the World Forum on Urban Forests in 2018. He acknowledged that before Bosco Verticale was built, there was skepticism about growing trees at great heights. He said that the critics didn't understand that nature and the built environment could work well together.

Boeri was right. Eight years after the treescrapers were completed, Bosco Verticale's trees were alive and well. So were the many birds and other animals that made their homes on the towers. But that doesn't mean that vertical forests can't have problems. For example, China's first vertical forest, Qiyi City Forest Garden in Chengdu, had a difficult launch in 2018. Building managers did not properly prune and care for the plants and trees on balconies on the development's eight towers. The balconies quickly became overgrown. To make matters worse, swarms of mosquitoes used the plants and trees as a breeding ground, and the bugs loved biting tower residents sitting on their tree-covered balconies. Because of these problems, residents were slow to move in. Since then building managers have stepped up plant maintenance and unspecified pest control and the towers are filling with contented urban forest dwellers.

## ECO-GENTRIFICATION

People who promote green architecture say that green buildings make urban life better. But are urban greening projects better for all city residents or just some of them? People living in and near green buildings benefit from cleaner air, less noise, and shading. But there is a darker side to green development. Urban ecologist Sarah Dooling, executive director of the Massachusetts Climate Action Network, uses the term *eco-gentrification* to describe one downside of green development.

Often, when developers build projects in urban neighborhoods, they buy existing old homes and either demolish or renovate them. The people already living there usually must move elsewhere. After the neighborhood is restored and redeveloped, with state-of-the-art new houses and buildings, the homes are often too expensive and property taxes are too high for those who formerly lived in the area. More affluent people move in, and poorer people leave. This is called gentrification. Eco-gentrification is when this happens with green development.

Eco-gentrification has occurred with many urban greening projects, including Bosco Verticale. The towers were part of a larger redevelopment of Milan's Porta Nuova area. Prior to 2004, when the Bosco Verticale project began, the area had affordable housing and a mostly working-class population. In 2007 developers started to demolish existing buildings in the area despite the protests of local residents. The residents did not succeed in stopping the project. They had to move to make way for new buildings, including UniCredit Tower, the tallest building in Italy, and Bosco Verticale. By 2017 Porta Nuova had become the richest district of any city in Europe. Its previous residents can no longer afford to live there.

Green projects like High Line Park can lead to eco-gentrification, when newly greened neighborhoods become too expensive for their former residents.

# Library of Trees

The Library of Trees (Biblioteca degli Alberi Milano), developed by Dutch landscape designer Petra Blaisse, sits on 24 acres (10 ha) at the foot of Bosco Verticale. The horizontal green space boasts five hundred trees that form twenty-two circular "forests." Each circle has a specific tree species. The design allows for water to flow into the ground beneath it, helping prevent damaging runoff that occurs in areas where there is primarily pavement. Park visitors can spend time within the circles—reading, resting, practicing yoga, or having picnics. The park also includes paths, open spaces, ninety thousand plants, a playground, and a dog park. Stones sitting alongside paths through the park are inscribed with the names of plants and even poems. One reads, "Un albero è un amico silenzioso," which in English means, "A tree is a silent friend."

Eco-gentrification also occurred in the development of New York's High Line Park. Although buildings were not demolished, the property values around the High Line increased 103 percent after the park opened. Wealthier people moved in, and many landlords raised the rent on apartments. Many lower-income residents moved out because the neighborhood became too expensive.

## GREEN BUILDINGS FOR EVERYONE

In response to eco-gentrification, some communities are building more affordable vertical forests. One is Boeri's nineteen-floor Trudo Vertical Forest designed for the city of Eindhoven in the Netherlands. The 125 apartments there are affordable and rent-controlled, so by law, landlords must keep the rents low.

Who decides whether projects such as Trudo Vertical Forest are built? Who decides about parks, tree planting, green infrastructure, and other efforts to improve city life? Lawmakers, developers, community organizations, and city residents all have a voice. "We need to have cities on board, politicians on board, we also need to have the general public on board helping us promote the importance of trees and also pushing their politicians to do better for trees," said Cecil Konijnendijk, a professor of urban forestry at the University of British Columbia in 2018.

Boeri takes this idea further to encompass using green architecture in the fight against climate change. He ended his 2018 "City Vision" presentation by explaining that in the fight against climate change, fear is a bad motivator. Rather than frighten people with warnings about rising sea levels, excessive heat, and weather disasters, we should talk about the positive things we can do to help the planet. These include planting more trees, protecting wild lands and wildlife, and making our cities greener.

Kids in Los Angeles plant trees in a park that was damaged by wildfire.

# CHAPTER 10

# Make a Difference in Your City

**We're living during an era of urban transformation.** Architects, botanists, and city planners are stepping up to make our cities greener. You might want to explore a career in one of those fields. But you don't have to be an architect or a botanist to make a difference. Everyone can get involved in their community, no matter what their age. You can do many things to make an impact and encourage urban greening projects in your city.

## VOLUNTEER YOUR TIME

Consider volunteering at a local botanical garden. Assist staffers, weed and mulch garden beds, lead visitors on tours, or do other jobs that help keep the garden running. Look for volunteer opportunities geared just to teens. For instance, the High School Explainer Program at the

New York Botanical Garden lets teenage volunteers teach visitors about the garden's plants and programs. You can volunteer at a city park too. Jobs might include planting trees, picking up litter, and maintaining flower beds. Contact your city park office, and ask where and how you can help. Some parks have a "friends of the park" group that would welcome your assistance. Your volunteer experience will help your community and teach you valuable skills. It might even lead you to a career in botany, urban forestry, or other work involving plants.

## JOIN A COMMUNITY GARDEN

Urban community gardens transform vacant lots into living green spaces that can support biodiversity and provide food for area residents. Urban gardens also make cities healthier, with improved air quality and fresh food for gardeners and community members. As a volunteer, you might help plant and harvest vegetables, weed garden beds, load produce into containers, or do community outreach. Search online to find a community garden near you. You might also check with your city for help finding an existing garden. If you can't find one where you live, talk to your friends, family members, neighbors, and teachers about starting your own.

### Adopt a Pocket Park

Small urban parks, often called pocket parks for their size, can be found in many city neighborhoods. They grew in popularity in Europe and the United States after World War II. If you have a pocket park in your neighborhood, consider adopting it. Help keep it clean. Care for the plants that grow there. Brainstorm ways you can encourage your neighbors to enjoy the park.

## GET INVOLVED IN DECISION-MAKING

Kids use parks more than adults do, so it makes sense that kids should have a voice in park design and development. To find out what's planned for parks in your area or to propose a new park program, contact your city parks department or city planning department. Examine your community. Are there vacant lots that can be turned into community gardens or parks? Would a community building be a good spot for a public park or a living wall? Talk to school friends, neighbors, and neighborhood business owners about urban greening ideas. What projects would they like to see? Are they willing to get involved in the project? Once you have support for a project, create a proposal to submit to local government officials.

Health in the Hood founder Asha Walker helps two teens plant their community garden.

## Turn Your Community Green

How can you help green your city or town? To get started, follow these steps:

- Explore the green areas around your school or community and make a chart of existing green spaces, such as parks, tree-lined streets, green roofs, and living walls.
- Note areas for improvement. Are there vacant lots that can be turned into community gardens? Are any properties good candidates for adding green roofs or living walls? Make a list of your findings.
- Survey neighbors and business owners about urban greening ideas. What would they like to see? Are they willing to get involved with projects?
- Review all the data from the finished survey and create a proposal to submit to your local planning department.

## GROW AN INDOOR GARDEN

You don't need a big building to create an indoor garden. You can make one inside your own home. Planting veggies and herbs indoors saves on trips to the supermarket, which means using less gas and reducing carbon emissions. This small action helps the entire planet, and you get fresh food. It's a win-win. Place growing plants near windows so they get sunlight. If you get minimal light coming through the windows, purchase light bulbs designed specifically for indoor growing. If you want help setting up a home garden, visit a local nursery and talk to the staff there. They'll tell you about proper plant containers, lighting, watering, and which plants grow well indoors.

# Tree Mail

You've heard of email and snail mail, but how about tree mail? One city thought of a clever way for let residents report on the condition of city trees. Since 2013 Melbourne has given trees their own email addresses. They also have identification numbers, which help residents communicate with and about specific trees. As the city intended, many residents use the emails to update city workers about problems with certain trees, such as fallen branches. But these messages have gone beyond reporting on problems. Many residents have conversations with their local trees (with the help of city workers). Here's an example:

> Dear Green Leaf Elm, Tree ID 1022165
> I hope you like living at St. Mary's. Most of the time I like it too.
> I have exams coming up and I should be busy studying. You do
> not have exams because you are a tree. I don't think that there
> is much more to talk about as we don't have a lot in common,
> you being a tree and such. But I'm glad we're in this together.

The tree's reply:

> Hello F,
> I do like living here.
> I hope you do well in your exams. Research has shown that
> nature can influence the way people learn in a positive way, so
> I hope I inspire your learning.
>
> > Best wishes,
> > Green Leaf Elm, Tree ID 102216541

Reach out to local officials in your areas to propose starting a similar program through social media where you live.

You can help fight climate change by planting trees.

## PLANT A TREE

Planting native trees is one of the best things people can do to fight climate change. Many organizations help people plant trees in their neighborhoods. To find a tree-planting project in your area, contact your local parks department. Or search the name of your town or city and "tree planting" online. You can also volunteer to help care for trees that have already been planted in your community. Call your government offices to find out how to get involved.

## A NEW PERSPECTIVE

Planting a tree or growing a garden in your city is a small step, but when many people take small steps, they can go a long way. Anything you do to make your world greener is a step in the right direction. In our quickly changing, climate-challenged planet, connecting with nature becomes more important each day.

"We all have to reconcile nature and [humans] to a much greater degree," says living wall–designer Blanc. "Simply because we have no alternative. Now more than half the people of the world are living in towns and most of human beings have now lost all contacts with nature, but people all over the world are still very interested [in] natural environments."

Australian architect Amanda Sturgeon suggests that humans take an entirely new perspective on human-built and natural environments. She says that rather than view our surroundings as places for people, roads, and buildings, with some areas set aside for trees and plants, we should view our surroundings as places for trees, plants, and wildlife, with some areas set aside for human use. With that outlook, she says, "we will have a chance at bringing people and nature into a healthy balance."

# GLOSSARY

**aeroponics:** a plant-growing method in which roots hang down below a shelf or inside a tall hollow column, where they are misted with nutrient-rich water

**afforestation:** establishing a forest on land where a forest never grew before

**aquaponics:** a system in which fish and food plants are grown in separate tanks of water, with fish waste providing nutrients for the growing plants

**arborist:** a specialist in the care and maintenance of trees

**biodiversity:** a variety of plant and animal species living together in a specific place

**biophilia:** the enjoyment of being around other living organisms

**botanical garden:** a garden designed for the growth, study, and exhibition of plants of a specific type or a specific place

**botany:** a branch of biology dealing with plant life

**climate change:** a warming of Earth due to increased levels of carbon dioxide in the atmosphere, caused by the burning of fossil fuels

**deforestation:** the loss of a forest, often occurring when people cut or burn down trees to make room for farms, ranches, homes, roads, and industry

**ecosystem:** a community of interdependent living and nonliving things, including plants, animals, air, soil, and water

**evaporation:** the change from a liquid or solid into a gas

**extinct:** having no living members. A species becomes extinct when the last individual of that species dies.

**fertilizer:** a substance added to soil, such as manure or a chemical mixture, that provides extra nutrients to plants

**food desert:** a neighborhood or area without stores selling healthy food

**fungi:** organisms that obtain food by absorbing it from other living things. Some fungi can harm crops.

**greenhouse gas:** a gas, such as carbon dioxide, that traps heat in the atmosphere

**habitat:** the natural home of a living thing, where it can find food, shelter, and mates for reproduction

heat island: an urban area that is a lot warmer than the surrounding countryside because of human activities and structures

herbicide: a substance used to kill weeds growing alongside crops

horticulture: the art and practice of growing and maintaining a garden

hydroponics: a system for growing plants in tanks of water

insulation: material that keeps heat, sound, or electric current from flowing from one area to another

irrigation: a system of pipes, pumps, or other equipment for moving water from one place to another

monoculture: growing only one type of crop on a piece of land

nursery: a business or facility that germinates and grows plants, which might be sold to landscapers, home gardeners, farmers, or others

organic farming: growing crops without chemical pesticides, herbicides, or fertilizers

pesticide: a substance used to kill harmful insects

photosynthesis: when green plants combine sunlight, carbon dioxide, and water to make food

pollinate: to transfer pollen between the reproductive organs of flowering plants, enabling plants to make seeds

smog: fog made heavier and darker by air pollution, or polluting gases in the air that are chemically changed by sunlight. The term is a combination of *smoke* and *fog.*

solar panel: a plate or other device that collects sunlight to be converted into heat or electricity, or stored in a battery

species: a group of living things of the same type. Male and female members of the same species can mate with one another and produce offspring.

transpiration: the passage of water from a living thing, such as a tree leaf, into the atmosphere

urban forestry: caring for trees growing in a city

vertical: reaching upward toward the sky instead of stretching horizontally, or side to side

# SOURCE NOTES

4   Rex Weyler, "A Brief History of Environmentalism," Greenpeace, January 5, 2018, https://www.greenpeace.org/international/story/11658/a-brief-history-of-environmentalism.

6   "Why Cities Are Mankind's Greatest Invention," *Marketplace*, February 17, 2011, https://www.marketplace.org/2011/02/17/why-cities-are-mankinds-greatest-invention.

9   "City Vision: Vertical Forests," New York Times Events, December 7, 2018, YouTube video, 12:11, https://youtu.be/wa_-3FrPIIs.

9   "After the Renowned Vertical Forest in Milan, the Concept of Urban Forestry by Architect Stefano Boeri Spreads in Northern Europe, Starting from Eindhoven, Utrecht and Antwerp," *Business Wire*, May 7, 2021, https://www.businesswire.com/news/home/20210507005177/en/After-the-Renowned-Vertical-Forest-in-Milan-the-Concept-of-Urban-Forestry-by-Architect-Stefano-Boeri-Spreads-in-Northern-Europe-Starting-From-Eindhoven-Utrecht-and-Antwerp.

16   Lisa K. Bates, ed., "Race and Spatial Imaginary," *Planning Theory and Practice* 19, no. 2 (2018), https://www.tandfonline.com/doi/full/10.1080/14649357.2018.1456816.

16   "Rewriting the Future of Our Cities," Fiat, June 4, 2021, YouTube video, 33:33, https://www.youtube.com/watch?v=wnn6y8MkXd8.

16   "After the Renowned Vertical Forest in Milan."

18   "Essay: History of Urban Forests," Forest History.org, accessed March 9, 2022, https://foresthistory.org/wp-content/uploads/2017/01/7studentPages.pdf.

24   Shubhendu Sharma, "How to Grow a Forest in Your Backyard," Ted@BCG Paris, May 2016, https://www.ted.com/talks/shubhendu_sharma_how_to_grow_a_forest_in_your_backyard#t-69296.

24   "More Greening in Darwin," Mirage, June 16, 2021, https://www.miragenews.com/more-greening-in-darwin-578620/.

25   Madeleine Wedesweiler, "The World's Five Coolest Vertical Forests," *Domain*, February 9 2017, https://www.domain.com.au/news/the-worlds-five-coolest-vertical-forests-20170207-gu7jhv/.

26   "The Life of Frank Lloyd Wright," Frank Lloyd Wright Foundation, accessed March 9, 2022, https://franklloydwright.org/frank-lloyd-wright.

26   "Frank Lloyd Wright Inspiration," Form and Function, November 7, 2018, https://formandfunctiondesign.com/frank-lloyd-wright-inspiration.

26   "Frank Lloyd Wright and Nature," Guggenheim, accessed March 9, 2022, https://www.guggenheim.org/teaching-materials/the-architecture-of-the-solomon-r-guggenheim-museum/frank-lloyd-wright-and-nature.

27   "Urban Forestry," Stefano Boeri Architetti, March 1, 2022, https://www.stefanoboeriarchitetti.net/en/urban-forestry.

29   "Vertical Forest Inspirations," Stefano Boeri Architetti, May 5, 2018, https://www.stefanoboeriarchitetti.net/en/vertical-forest-en/ispirazioni-bosco-verticale-tre.

30   Friedensreich Hundertwasser, "Forestation of the City," Hundertwasser, 2022, https://hundertwasser.com/en/texts/verwaldung_der_staedte.

30   "Un albero di trenta piani," Lyrics Translate, accessed March 9, 2022, https://lyricstranslate.com/en/un-albero-di-trenta-piani-tree-thirty-floors.html.

31   "Vertical Forest Inspirations."

32   Thomas Banbury, "The Suburbs of Hell: 500 Years of Polluted Air in London," *Era*, February 2, 2021, https://era-magazine.com/2021/02/02/the-suburbs-of-hell-500-years-of-polluted-air-in-london/.

34   "Vertical Forest Inspirations #Two," Stefano Boeri Architetti, May 6, 2018, https://www.stefanoboeriarchitetti.net/en/vertical-forest-en/vertical-forest-inspirations-two/.

35   "Vertical Forest Inspirations #Two."

35   "Boeri and the Bosco Verticale," Effebiquattro, November 20, 2017, http://www.effebiquattro.it/en/boeri-bosco-verticale-effebiquattro/.

38   Daniele Belleri, "The Secrets of Vertical Forests," Studio Laura Gatti, April 19, 2018, http://areademo.net/lauragatti/i-segreti-del-bosco-verticale/?lang=en.

38   Belleri, "The Secrets of Vertical Forests."

43   Anmar Frangoul, "A 'Mutant Building' in Milan Is Saving Energy and Pleasing Residents," CNBC, November 27, 2020, https://www.cnbc.com/2020/11/26/a-mutant-building-in-milan-is-saving-energy-and-pleasing-residents.html.

43 Amy Frearson, "Stefano Boeri's 'Vertical Forest' Nears Completion in Milan," Dezeen, May 15, 2014, https://www.dezeen.com/2014/05/15/stefano-boeri-bosco-verticale-vertical-forest-milan-skyscrapers/.

45 "Visual Soundscapes—Cities," BBC America, August 23, 2017, https://www.youtube.com/watch?v=MCIlDZ-6bnA.

46 Laura Gatti, "Why We All Should Be Gardeners in the Eco-Cities of the Future," filmed May 23, 2014, TEDx video, 14:24, https://www.youtube.com/watch?v=0J64B37FAqw.

47 "Italy's High-Rise Forests Take Root around the World," News24, October 8, 2017, https://www.news24.com/news24/Green/News/italys-high-rise-forests-take-root-around-the-world-20171008.

49 Etienne Benson, "The Urbanization of the Eastern Gray Squirrel in the United States," *Journal of American History* 100, no. 3 (December 2013): 642–644, http://etiennebenson.com/wp-content/uploads/2013/11/benson-2013-jah-squirrels.pdf.

57 Carina Weijma, "Green Towers, and Rooftop Fields, Not a Luxury but a Smart Investment," Innovation Origins, June 5, 2021, https://innovationorigins.com/en/green-towers-and-rooftop-meadows-not-a-luxury-but-a-smart-investment/.

60 "Rare Orchids Found in City of London Bank's Rooftop Garden," BBC News, June 15, 2021, https://www.bbc.com/news/uk-england-london-57439921.

63 Spencer Fletcher (@Spencerfletch0), "It's World Green Roof Day," Twitter, June 5, 2021, 11:25 p.m., https://twitter.com/Spencerfletch0/status/1401424869355630593.

68 Jade McSorley, "An Interview with Architect Patrick Blanc," *Twenty6*, November 22, 2017, http://www.twenty6magazine.com/issue-m/lifestyle/interview-architect-patrick-blanc.

69 Patrick Blanc, "Stefano Boeri in Dialogue with Patrick Blanc," filmed November 30, 2018, World Forum on Urban Forests video, 53:56, Facebook, https://www.facebook.com/StefanoBoeriArchitetti/videos/patrick-blanc-the-greens-and-the-greys-the-life-of-plants-that-colonize-vertical/340558766524528/.

69–70 Rebecca Leber, "How to Redesign Cities to Withstand Heat Waves," Vox, June 30, 2021, https://www.vox.com/22557563/how-to-redesign-cities-for-heat-waves-climate-change.

84 Tim De Chant, "Can We Please Stop Drawing Trees on Top of Skyscrapers?" *Per Square Mile*, July 17, 2020, https://persquaremile.com/2013/03/07/trees-dont-like-it-up-there/.

85 "Fiat: Rewriting the Future of Our Cities," *Facebook Watch*, January 20, 2022, https://www.facebook.com/Fiat/videos /507050080497832/.

89 Tommaso Perrone, "What We Learned from the World Forum on Urban Forests 2018 in Mantova," Lifegate, December 3, 2018, https://www.lifegate.com/mantova-wfuf2018-2.

95 Adrienne LaFrance, "When You Give a Tree an Email Address," *Atlantic*, accessed March 9, 2022, https://www.theatlantic.com /technology/archive/2015/07/when-you-give-a-tree-an-email-address /398210/.

97 McSorley, "An Interview with Architect Patrick Blanc."

97 Amanda Sturgeon, Rewilding Our Cities: Beauty, Biodiversity and the Biophilic Cities Movement," *Guardian*, April 4, 2021, https:// www.theguardian.com/artanddesign/2021/apr/05/re-wilding-our -cities-beauty-biodiversity-and-the-biophilic-cities-movement.

## SELECTED BIBLIOGRAPHY

Boeri, Stefano. *A Vertical Forest*. Mantova, Italy: Corraini Edizioni, 2015.

Brooks Pfeiffer, Bruce, and Gerald Nordland, eds. *Frank Lloyd Wright: In the Realm of Ideas*. Carbondale: Southern Illinois University Press, 1988.

Dion, Mark. *High Line of the Borough of Manhattan*. New York: Printed Matter, 2013.

Hall, Damon M., Gerardo R. Camilo, Rebecca K. Tonietto, Jeff Ollerton, Karin Ahrné, Mike Arduser, John S. Ascher, et al. "The City as a Refuge for Insect Pollinators." The Society for Conservation Biology. *Conservation Biology* 31, no. 1 (September 14, 2016): 24–29. https://conbio.onlinelibrary .wiley.com/doi/10.1111/cobi.12840.

Jordan, Michael. *Urban Arboreal: A Modern Glossary of City Trees*. London: White Lion, 2018.

Konijnendijk, Cecil. *The Forest and the City: The Cultural Landscape of Urban Woodland*. Cham, Switzerland: Springer, 2018.

Lydon, Patrick M. "A City Designed by Trees," The Nature of Cities, September 12, 2018. https://www.thenatureofcities.com/2018/09/12 /city-designed-trees.

McBride, Joe. *The World's Urban Forests: History, Composition, Design, Function and Management*. Cham, Switzerland: Springer, 2017.

Nitoslawski, Sophie, Nadine Galle, Cecil Konijnendijk van den Bosch, and James Steenberg. "Smarter Ecosystems for Smarter Cities? A Review of Trends, Technologies, and Turning Points for Smart Urban Forestry." *Sustainable Cities and Society* 51 (November 2019). https://doi.org/10.1016/j.scs.2019.101770.

Pakenham, Thomas. *Remarkable Trees of the World*. New York: W. W. Norton, 2003.

Park, Hyeone, Moritz Kramer, Jeanine M. Rhemtulla, and Cecil C. Konijnendijk. "Urban Food Systems That Involve Trees in Northern America and Europe. *Urban Forestry and Urban Greening* 45 (October 2019). https://doi.org/10.1016/j.ufug.2019.06.003.

Wohlleben, Peter. *The Hidden Life of Trees*. Vancouver, BC: Greystone Books, 2016.

World Health Organization. "Urban Green Spaces and Health: A Review of Evidence." WHO, 2016. https://www.euro.who.int/__data/assets/pdf_file/0005/321971/Urban-green-spaces-and-health-review-evidence.pdf.

Yao, Na, Cecil Konijnendijk van den Bosch, Jun Yang, Tahia Devisscher, Zach Wirtz, Liming Jia, Jie Duan, and Lvyi Ma. "Beijing's 50 Million New Urban Trees: Strategic Governance for Large-Scale Urban Afforestation." *Urban Forestry and Urban Greening* 44 (August 2019). https://doi.org/10.1016/j.ufug.2019.126392.

# FURTHER INFORMATION

## Books

Blevins, Wiley. *Ninja Plants: Survival and Adaptation in the Plant World*. Minneapolis: Twenty-First Century Books, 2017.

Hirsch, Rebecca. *Where Have All the Bees Gone?* Minneapolis: Twenty-First Century Books, 2020.

Hughes, Meredith Sayles. *Plants vs. Meat: The Health, History, and Ethics of What We Eat*. Minneapolis: Twenty-First Century Books, 2016.

Koch, Melissa. *Forest Talk: How Trees Communicate*. Minneapolis: Twenty-First Century Books, 2019.

Mihaly, Christy, and Sue Heavenrich. *Diet for a Changing Climate: Food for Thought*. Minneapolis: Twenty-First Century Books, 2019.

Peterson, Christy. *Earth Day and the Environmental Movement: Standing Up for Earth*. Minneapolis: Twenty-First Century Books, 2020.

Swanson, Jennifer. *Geoengineering Earth's Climate*. Minneapolis: Twenty-First Century Books, 2018.

Willkens, Danielle S. *Architecture for Teens: A Beginner's Book for Aspiring Architects*. Emeryville, CA: Rockridge, 2021.

Wohlleben, Peter. *Can You Hear the Trees Talking? Discovering the Hidden Life of the Forest*. Vancouver, BC: Greystone Kids, 2020.

## Websites

AeroFarms
https://www.aerofarms.com
A leader in indoor farming, AeroFarms employs cutting-edge technology to grow pesticide-free leafy greens. Check out the website to learn how it's done.

Akira Miyawaki
http://akiramiyawaki.com
Learn how the Japanese botanist devised a technique for quickly growing dense stands of trees—a method he's applied around the world.

Earth Day
https://www.earthday.org
The first Earth Day was in 1970. Since then the Earth Day organization has been leading the effort for environmental protection.

European Federation of Green Roofs and Walls
https://efb-greenroof.eu
Europe is a leader in the movement to create living walls and roofs. This website offers news, information, and lots of pictures.

Health in the Hood
https://www.healthinthehood.org
This group uses community gardens to fight hunger and food deserts in Miami, Florida.

Homegrown National Park
https://homegrownnationalpark.org
This organization encourages people to restore biodiversity and regenerate ecosystems by planting native species on their own land—even in their own backyards.

Letchworth Garden City Heritage Foundation
  https://www.letchworth.com
  Created in the early twentieth century, Letchworth, England, is a green
  city designed by urban planner Sir Ebenezer Howard.

National Wildlife Federation
  http://nwf.org
  The federation works to protect endangered species, restore wildlife
  habitats, and inspire people to work hand in hand with the natural world.

New York City Street Tree Map
  https://tree-map.nycgovparks.org
  Here you can learn about the trees of New York City and even find out
  about individual trees.

The Spheres
  https://www.seattlespheres.com
  Learn about this innovative green workspace for Amazon employees,
  home to more than forty thousand plants from forests around the world.

Stefano Boeri Architetti
  https://www.stefanoboeriarchitetti.net
  Learn more about Bosco Verticale and other green buildings designed by
  Stefano Boeri.

Vertical Garden Patrick Blanc
  https://www.verticalgardenpatrickblanc.com
  Blanc has built living walls around the world. See pictures of his creations
  and learn about his work here.

## PLACES TO EXPLORE

You might live near one of the green buildings or farms on this list. If so, talk to a
teacher, parent, or other adult about arranging a visit. Even if you can't visit, you
can still look for these places online to find lots of pictures and more information.

### Green Buildings and Structures

Bosco Verticale, Porto Nuova, Milan, Italy
Fallingwater, Mill Run, Pennsylvania
High Line, New York, New York
One Central Park, Sydney, Australia

## Green Roofs

American Society of Landscape Architects, Washington, DC
Berkshire Botanical Garden, Stockbridge, Massachusetts
Biesbosch Museum, Werkendam, the Netherlands
Bus stops, Flint, Michigan
Bus stops, Kuala Lumpur, Malaysia
Bus stops, Philadelphia, Pennsylvania
Bus stops, Utrecht, the Netherlands
Brooklyn Botanic Garden Visitor Center, New York, New York
College of Agriculture, Urban Sustainability and Environmental Sciences,
    University of the District of Columbia, Washington, DC
Chongqing Taoyuanju Community Center, Chongqing, China
Daniel F. and Ada L. Rice Plant Conservation Science Center, Chicago, Illinois
Espace Bienvenüe, Marne-la-Vallée, France
Meera Sky Garden House, Singapore, Singapore
Moesgaard Museum, Aarhus, Denmark
Moore Farms Botanical Garden, Lake City, South Carolina
Olympic Sculpture Park, Seattle, Washington
Padua Botanical Garden, Padua, Italy
Public buses, Singapore, Singapore
Städel Museum, Frankfurt, Germany

## Living Walls

Athenaeum Hotel, London, United Kingdom
Birmingham-Shuttlesworth International Airport, Birmingham, Alabama
Britomart Greenwall, Auckland, New Zealand
CaixaForum, Madrid, Spain
Del Amo Fashion Center, Los Angeles, California
Detroit Metropolitan Airport, Detroit, Michigan
Drew School, San Francisco, California
Ed Lumley Centre for Engineering Innovation, Windsor, Canada
Ellerman House, Cape Town, South Africa
George Bush Intercontinental Airport, Houston, Texas
Grand Palladium Costa Mujeres Resort and Spa, Cancún, Mexico
LaGuardia Airport, New York, New York
Miami International Airport, Miami, Florida
Moore Farms Botanical Garden, Lake City, South Carolina
Musée du quai Branly, Paris, France
Nature Lab, Rhode Island School of Design, Providence, Rhode Island
New Orleans Botanical Garden, New Orleans, Louisiana

Oberoi Gurgaon Hotel, Gurgaon, India
Prudential Tower Living Wall, Newark, New Jersey
Seattle-Tacoma International Airport, Seattle, Washington
St. Louis Lambert International Airport, St. Louis, Missouri
Worth Avenue, Palm Beach, Florida

## Urban Farms

Battery Urban Farm, New York, New York
Brooklyn Grange, Brooklyn, New York
Chicago Lights Urban Farm, Chicago, Illinois
Edible Gardens, Lincoln Park Zoo, Chicago Illinois
Farm LA, Los Angeles, California
GrowNYC Teaching Garden, Governors Island, New York
La Finca del Sur Community Garden, Bronx, New York
O'Hare International Airport, Chicago, Illinois
Step Up on Vine, Hollywood, California

# CALENDAR OF EVENTS

**March 21** **International Day of Forests.** Forests are home to about 80 percent of the world's biodiversity. This holiday brings awareness to the value and preservation of all kinds of forests around the world.

**April** **Arbor Day.** This holiday celebrates trees and tree planting in the United States. It usually falls on the last Friday in April. It is commemorated by planting trees.

**May 22** **World Biodiversity Day.** Established by the United Nations, this event calls attention to the need to increase and protect biodiverse ecosystems.

**June 5** **World Environment Day.** First celebrated in 1974, this is a day to raise awareness about the threats to our natural environment and programs to help protect it.

**June 6** **World Green Roof Day.** Started by European green roof organizations, this day was first observed in 2021.

**October 10** **National Walk to a Park Day.** This event encourages people to walk to local parks, use parks, and work to build more of them.

# INDEX

## PHOTO ACKNOWLEDGMENTS

## ACKNOWLEDGMENTS

It goes without saying that I send out my sincere thanks to the planners and speakers of the FAO World Forum of Urban Forests. I could not have hoped for a more informative gathering of worldwide green urban professionals. Much gratitude to Dr. Cecil Konijnendijk, Patrick Blanc, and the other speakers. The sessions were enlightening and informative, and they formed the basis for this book. Un'abbondanza di ringraziamenti alla gente di Mantova per averci accolto cosi' bene. Inoltre, molte grazie a Stefano Boeri e al suo team.

In addition, my gratitude extends to Shaina Olmanson, the entire Twenty-First Century team headed by Shaina Olmanson, agent extraordinaire Jennifer Laughran, and my writing buddies, Lois Huey and Anita Sanchez, for their early reads. Lastly, this book was a joy to research because my husband, Dean, accompanied me to the world forum. It was his love of espresso that led me to my serendipitous meeting with Stefano Boeri. Mille grazie tutti!

## ABOUT THE AUTHOR

Nancy F. Castaldo has written nonfiction children's books about our planet for more than twenty years, including Junior Library Guild selection and Green Earth Book Award title *The Story of Seeds* and her most recent Junior Library Guild selection for young adults *When the World Runs Dry*. As an environmental educator, Castaldo hopes to empower young readers with her books about the earth. Her interest in vertical forests started during a trip to Italy when she heard about the visionary design of Bosco Verticale. She is based in New York's Hudson Valley. Learn more about Nancy and her books at www.nancycastaldo.com.